Theology
for
Today's
Catholic

A Handbook

An Introduction to
Adult Theological Reflection

STEPHEN T. REHRAUER, C.SS.R.

Liguori
ONE LIGUORI DRIVE
LIGUORI MO 63057-9999

Imprimi Potest:
Thomas D. Picton, C.Ss.R.
Provincial, Denver Province
The Redemptorists

Imprimatur:
Most Reverend Robert J. Hermann
Auxiliary Bishop
Archdiocese of St. Louis

ISBN 0-7648-1308-0
Library of Congress Catalog Card Number: 2005931492

© 2005, Liguori Publications
Printed in the United States of America
05 06 07 08 09 5 4 3 2 1

Liguori Publications, a nonprofit corporation, is an apostolate of the Redemptorists. To learn more about the Redemptorists, visit Redemptorists.com.

To order, call 1-800-325-9521
www.liguori.org

Contents

Introduction

S everal years ago, while flying cross-country to visit my sister, I had the privilege of sitting next to a young woman with whom I struck up a casual conversation. As the topic turned to what each of us does for a living, and I told her that I'm a priest and a theologian teaching in Rome, the conversation took a serious turn for the better. She told me that she is a very active evangelical Christian, deeply committed to her church and very involved in its activities. She then began asking me questions about the Catholic religion; questions that had been puzzling her for years about why we Catholics do many of the things that we do. As I answered her questions one after another, explaining the theological reasons why we venerate the Blessed Mother and the saints, confess our sins to the priest, wear medals, go to Communion so often, as well as the spiritual meanings behind these and the dozens of other traditional Catholic practices, she expressed her amazement. She told me I was the first Catholic with whom she had spoken who was able to give her a real answer to her questions. None of her other Catholic friends had ever been able to explain the reasons behind their faith practices. Their answers had always been of the character, "That's just what we're taught to do," or "Because that's what the pope said we're supposed to do." She told me that now, as a result of our conversation, she was going to have to rethink her whole attitude toward the Catholic faith. She now understood that our practices were in fact deeply rooted in the Bible, and profoundly religious in a truly Christian way.

I was grateful to God for having been placed next to that woman that day. We each had the opportunity to be a source of God's grace to each other. But I also found my experience with that young woman disquieting. It immediately brought to mind a similar personal experience I had years earlier when I was invited to preach a day of recollection to a small group of Catholics involved in the charismatic renewal. They had asked me to preach on the meaning of salvation. When I arrived, I was amazed to discover there were five hundred Catholics waiting to hear what I had to say about salvation. I began by asking for a show of hands. How many people here want to be saved? All of the hands immediately went up. Then I asked the second question. How many people here have been saved? More than half of the hands went down. The third question followed. How many here can tell me exactly what it means to be saved? All of the hands went down. Here is an all too common problem with our faith. We know what to believe. We do believe. But many of us find it difficult to explain what our beliefs mean in concrete or practical terms, or to actually put into words why exactly it is that we believe.

This may be because religious education for most of us was oriented to the reception of our basic sacraments. We identified the study of our faith and its meaning as something we had to do in order to get something else. Instead of learning that the study of our religion is important, necessary, and good in and of itself, we began to think of it almost as a necessary evil we had to undergo for the sake of something else we wanted. We may have come away with the false idea that having learned what was required for our sacraments, we now knew everything we needed to know in order to understand what our Catholic faith is. And so once we received our sacraments, we stopped studying.

Let's face it. Most of our religious education structures are geared to children. As children we may or may not have learned how to understand and make sense out of what we believe. If our religious education and the search for the meaning of our faith ends at the age of eight or twelve, with the reception of first Communion or confirmation, our faith understanding runs the risk of remaining that of an eight year old, even though we are now thirty, or forty, or fifty years old. When the full force of life hits us and we try to make sense out of what is going on inside of and around us, what we learned at the age of eight may not be of much help. We may even fall into the trap of thinking that religion is no longer very useful to us, or worse still, that our religion offers answers to questions that aren't ours, but doesn't provide answers to our own very real problems. Too many of us can identify with the Samaritan woman that Jesus met at the well in the fourth chapter of John's Gospel. We worship what we do not understand, rather than worshiping out of our understanding. Adult faith requires a constant search for a deeper and more mature understanding. As we live our lives, as our lives become busier and more complicated, our understanding of the meaning of what we believe, and what we do when we act on our beliefs, must also keep pace and grow. Christ comes to us in the Church precisely so that we can understand what we worship.

This handbook is about what and why we Catholics believe. The work is divided into three sections. The first section is about theology and the need for all followers of Christ to become theologians. The second section deals with the life, ministry, death, and resurrection of Jesus Christ, and how our understanding of Christ gives form and shape to our theology, revealing Jesus to be the answer to all of our faith questions. The third section is about the salvation that comes to us through Christ, what it requires of us personally, and the difference it makes in our lives and in our world.

This small book does not pretend to provide every possible answer to all possible questions. It merely tries to impress upon the reader the importance of asking the questions and seeking the answers throughout life. It also attempts to point the way to some of the important questions that adult Catholics ought to discern about their faith, and some ways in which adult Catholics can go about that. It does not attempt to summarize all of Catholic theology. It does try to help a Catholic come to a knowledge of the basic insights, principles, and ways in which Catholic theology tries to arrive at a deeper understanding of what we as a Church and as members of that Church believe and why. The reader, as he or she reads, will hopefully find himself or herself actually beginning to do theology. The questions raised and the theological points discussed will hopefully give birth to other and more personal questions for the readers, which will inspire them to seek the answers to their own theological questions through personal study, prayer and reflection.

Chapter One

ALL CHRISTIANS ARE CALLED TO BE THEOLOGIANS

There is a tendency at times, even among theologians, to identify theology with catechesis, as if the purpose of theology is to tell people what to believe about God, or to explain to interested nonbelievers what we Catholics believe. Catechism and theology are not the same thing. Theology is about understanding what we believe. Catechesis is about communicating the shared understanding of the experiences of faith we have in common as a Christian community. Theology should not be confused with official Church teaching. Official Church teaching contains theology and is based upon it, but theology can never be reduced to official teaching. In fact, unless one moves beyond the official teaching to understand the theology behind it and out of which it grows, it is very difficult to even appreciate the full depth and beauty of the truth that the official teachings communicate.

Theology is a profession in the Christian churches. One becomes a professional Catholic theologian in much the same way that one becomes any type of professional: by going to school, learning the basic principles and rules for doing theology, earning a degree, and eventually receiving an official mandate from the legitimate authority to teach in the name of the Catholic Church. Once the theologian begins researching, teaching, writing, or otherwise doing the work of the theologian, the works and writings produced are regularly examined by those in authority to ensure that the theologian remains in harmony with the Church's living theological tradition. The professional theologian is a competent and certified professional who loves the Catholic Church so much that he or she dedicates his or her life to serving the Church in its search for knowledge of the truth and in its mission to proclaim the good news of salvation.

1. All Theology Is Faith Searching for Understanding

But there is another understanding of theology which is much more ancient, and which is the foundation upon which the professional discipline is built. This basic meaning of theology is expressed in the first definition that students hear on the first day of their first introduction to a theology course. It comes from Saint Anselm, but he got it from Saint Augustine, who took it from the prophet Isaiah. Theology is "faith searching for understanding." It is in this sense of the word that all Christians are called, even required, to become theologians.

This definition expresses an important insight. If one does not believe in God, one cannot do theology. The Letter to the Hebrews says this quite eloquently: "…without faith it is impossible to please God, for whoever would approach him must believe that he exists and that he rewards those who seek him" (11:6). Turning this around, faith in search of understanding is not the lack of understanding in search of faith. Nobody finds faith by reading theology books. Unless one already believes, the theology found in books usually makes very little sense. Nor should one study theology in order to learn what to believe. Nonbelievers can speculate about God's existence, about the nature of religion, about problems of human life, goodness, evil, life and death. But if they don't have faith in God, they are not doing theology. Rather, they are searching for the faith that will make doing theology possible. Once one has received the gift of faith, however, one is compelled to search for the meaning of what faith reveals. This could be considered the test for whether one really has received the gift of faith: Does it lead me to ask the question, "What does this mean?"

The Faith Experience

Shared Christian experience teaches us that faith is a gift. We receive it. We don't earn it. It's not something we are convinced into. We can't make it happen. We experience it. It is mysterious, and it is powerful. Faith makes its appearance when we first become aware of the presence and activity of God in our life. The awareness may occur in many different ways, and come through many different avenues. For most of us it appears gradually, through a lengthy process which includes the presence of our family and friends, what we learn from them, the experiences we share with them, in coming face to face with our own actions and their consequences. For others the awareness comes suddenly, almost in a flash, and often at moments of crisis when one must face the choice of either beginning to believe or of despairing. Whatever the setting in which it appears, or the process God chooses in gifting us, the experience of faith presents itself as an invitation by God to believe, and to trust in God's continued goodness, presence, and care.

Once we experience this presence and activity of God in our lives, then that very experience calls out to us to make sense out of it, and raises the fundamental questions which form the pillars of our shared faith and religious practice. Again we read in the Letter to the Hebrews about what faith really is: "Faith is the assurance of things hoped for, the conviction of things not seen." (11:1). When we begin to believe, we realize that all we have been hoping for is now being accomplished. The first consequence of finding faith is an inner tension. We experience faith as a source of comfort, of inner peace and joy. There is a God, and God is involved in our lives. We are not alone. On the other hand, there is the realization that we don't really know this God, what God's presence means, how we should relate and respond to this gift of peace we have received. So faith also is experienced as a restlessness, a realization that there is so much more we need to learn, to do, to become. In this latter quality, faith also contains within itself its own solution, because faith also provides us with a vision which goes beyond the use of our eyes.

Faith as Search

Real consequences follow from this understanding of faith. The first has to do with understanding and knowledge themselves. If understanding is the test of knowledge, then faith is an experiential source of knowledge which drives us to seek a deeper understanding. I can know on one level that God exists because I have experienced God's presence and activity. But my knowledge of the fact is not really a mature knowledge until I understand what the presence and activity of God in my life means here and now. Since God is always present and active, the ongoing experience of God requires that the search of faith for understanding also continue throughout our entire life.

To appreciate this aspect of faith as knowledge in search of deeper understanding, we need to take a step back to an understanding of reality which has been almost lost in our contemporary world. True knowledge requires more than the mere understanding of how something works. A knowledge of purpose is also necessary. Being a Catholic does not consist in knowing how to do what Catholics do, or even in doing physically what Catholics do. Merely fulfilling one's obligation to go to Mass on Sunday, for example, does not make one a "good Catholic." Being Catholic also requires knowing and understanding what the Mass is, what it means and expresses, understanding why Catholics go to Mass together on Sunday, and participating regularly in the Mass in order to express and make real in our daily lives what the Mass represents and does for us. It requires an understanding and a choosing of the purpose for which the Mass exists. This is what faith is designed by God to do. It helps us understand the purposes of what we see and do. Faith reveals to us God's intention, God's will for us. God wants us to know happiness and to enter into intimate communion with him. Our beliefs and our practices as expressions of faith are designed to lead us into intimate relationship with God and the discovery of that happiness.

2. Theology Is a Way in Which Faith Understands

Faith is not just one more experience like any other. It is a new way of experiencing. This new way of "seeing" reveals things to us that we do not ordinarily see. These hidden things which faith reveals are not always extraordinary or supernatural. More often than not, faith enables us to see and recognize the presence and activity of God all around us and in the ordinary events of our day to day lives. This vision may be dim or cloudy at the beginning, but as faith continues to grow in understanding and in the realization of what is hoped for, the vision becomes brighter and clearer. Faith is a window into the deeper meaning of our everyday experience. As we become more adept at looking with the eyes of faith, and seeing the presence and activity of our God in this way, our everyday experience becomes a source for deeper faith.

Faith as a Personal Experience

Another consequence that arises from faith has to do with judging whether what we are seeing is real or merely the creation of our own imaginations or desires. There is always the danger with knowledge that we are deluding ourselves. A common question raised by people who first discover their faith, who begin having experiences of God's presence, is whether or not they are going crazy. It is a legitimate question, since the line between mental illness and religiosity is a fine one if measured merely by human standards. Many experiences which appear at first glance to be religious and supernatural are merely natural psychological phenomena which can be completely explained without any appeal to the supernatural. We do tend to see what we want to see, and we actively filter out aspects of our experience that are painful or unpleasant to us. Even when the experience of faith is real, we often interpret it to mean what is most convenient for us or in keeping with our current world view. We are very good at putting words into God's mouth that say what we wish God would say to us. For this reason, the understanding of faith at which we arrive must be "tested" by way of dialogue, sharing with others what we have "seen" and "heard."

Faith Is Never Private

Faith which is authentic can never be an individual isolated understanding. It is a shared, historical, and experiential source of knowledge which leads us into deeper relationship with others who are having and sharing the same experiences and arriving at the same understanding. Faith draws us out of and beyond ourselves and connects us to others. By coming together with others who have had the same or similar experiences of God's presence and activity in their lives, we together come to a clearer understanding of the truth contained in these realities. The fruit of this process is the shared creation of structures which enable us together to guide our search for faith's meaning. Catechisms, creeds, and official Church teachings are formulas, structures, and tools which we as members of a group sharing the same faith experience have invented to guide us in our search for understanding. They provide a framework of theological ideas and principles which guide us as we seek deeper understanding, and they protect us from falling into the specific mistakes and false understandings that people have made in the past while carrying out their search.

Faith and Reason

The visions of faith and reason may appear to contradict each other at times, but any real contradiction cannot endure. Faith is not irrational or antirational, since the search for understanding requires that faith be grounded in and explainable by human reason. Faith vision is something we think about and that has to make sense in order to be believed. We are human beings, not animals or plants. We are reasonable and reasoning beings. It is God's expectation that we give glory to our Creator by using our ability to reason to know and love God ever more fully. A belief which has been clearly demonstrated by reason to be false is not a worthy foundation for faith in a thinking, reasoning person. When faith and reason are properly used, they complement each other. Ultimately there are things revealed by faith which can not be fully explained or understood by reason. We are not all-knowing. Our power to reason and to know does have limits. All knowledge, even the most scientific knowledge, will eventually rest upon some beliefs. But the meaning and the practical consequences which flow from these incomplete understand-ings can be discovered through reasoning.

The Practice of Faith

Faith is not just something we seek to understand. It is also something we practice. In the practice of our faith we give expression to its meaning, so that our actions and our words are guided by the faith which gives rise to them. Because faith is a shared reality, we must practice it not only as individuals, but as a group of people who share the same gift from a loving God. The concrete things we do that identify us as Catholics have a faith perspective which lies behind them and are the reasons why we do these things. When we participate in our specifically Catholic practices intentionally, really meaning the theology that they express, then one of the results is that these expressions strengthen and deepen our faith. They provide us with new faith experiences which also seek deeper understanding. Faith in this sense becomes a virtue or habit. In the process of living our faith in concrete action, we move from being people who have faith and who are seeking understanding, to become people of faith who live their understanding and share their faith with others through the way they live.

Faith That Is "Christian"

Faith seeks the knowledge of God, but not just any old knowledge. Faith seeks knowledge of the truth about God, a knowledge which is worthy of trust. God is the source of all that is, the creator of all life. And so faith also raises questions about God's will and activity; questions about why God created this world, why things are the way they are, what the purpose and meaning of life is, what it means to be human. All theology seeks to know God more fully. Christian theology, though, seeks to know God by way of the person of Jesus Christ. Jesus lived and walked this earth. We have recorded the deeds of his life and his teaching. He is a part of our shared history as a human race. He is part of our own lived and shared experience. Faith enables us to see that this person Jesus is an especially effective and trustworthy way in which we can come to know God. Furthermore, faith reveals to us that this knowledge of God comes not only by knowing about Jesus, or by studying his words and deeds, but also by way of entering into a personal relationship with Jesus. It is not enough to know about Jesus. One must get to know him. By knowing him, we come to know God. And here we discover the ultimate and most important purpose of faith. We not only come to know and understand things about God. We enter into in a personal relationship with God. And it is this relationship, and this relationship alone, which brings us happiness, casts out fear, enables us to make sense out of our lives, sustains us in times of difficulty and doubt, enhances our ability to transform our deepest hopes and dreams into reality, and reveals to us what a wonderful thing it is to be fully human and fully alive.

At the heart of Christian theology is the belief that Jesus is the Son of God who has become human. Jesus also shows us the truth about what it is to be a human being, and about how to live in a fully human way. Christian faith seeks a deeper understanding of the nature of God, the meaning of human existence, and of the relationship between God and humanity as this relationship is explained in the life, death, and resurrection of Jesus the Christ. He himself told us that he came that we might have life, and have it to the full. Knowing him enables us to find the answers to the most important questions in life: Who is God? What does it mean to be human? Does life have meaning? What is our destiny? Why do things happen the way that they do? Are we alone? Does all of this end with death, or is there something more beyond? What makes us different from those who haven't found Christ? What does God ask of me here and now? All of our Catholic practices which flow out of this search express the answers that we as a Church have found and strengthen our faith in the truth of these answers. By putting the understanding that we have found in faith's searching into concrete practice the circle completes itself, as the practice of lived faith opens us to newer and deeper experiences of the faith which is its source.

3. The Theological Sources of Faith's Understanding

Where do we go to find the answers? How do we know God? How do we know Jesus Christ? The normal way to learn about anything or anyone is to look at their activity. Things and persons reveal themselves to us by way of our experience of them. When it comes to living beings, we know them by what they do. We know a tree by its fruit. We are able to distinguish a human being from other types of animals by the fact that humans are capable of rational thought and communication with language. We know people as individuals both by what they say and by what they do. Real knowledge of the person, however, requires a bit more than just knowing what that person has done or hearing the words. It requires knowing why the person did what was done, the intention and purpose behind the action, and what the person meant to communicate in choosing the words that were spoken. This latter aspect also requires knowledge of the emotional tone and force, the way in which the words are spoken, and the context in which they were spoken. One has to go beyond the activity and the words to discover the person behind them which is being expressed and revealed by these.

We know God in much the same way. God is revealed in the same way that any personal being reveals itself: in word and deed. But the meaning of those words and deeds don't become clear until we have the knowledge of relationship with God.

Sacred Scripture

The Catholic Church believes that God is revealed in two sources, the sacred Scripture (words) and the living Tradition of the Church (deeds). Historically, Tradition took center stage in Catholic theology. But the Second Vatican Council reminded us that Scripture must be the soul of theology. In keeping Scripture as the heart and soul of theology, theologians face some very challenging difficulties. The Scriptures, like all forms of communication, need to be interpreted. Because the Bible is a collection of books written over a period of hundreds of years, one needs to know the context, the background, and the purpose for which each of the books was written in order to understand the original message. This type of research is painstaking, and takes a great deal of time and effort.

Knowing what the original message of the scriptural text is though, is not enough. God continues to speak to us today through the Scriptures. So, it is necessary to relate the original message to other historical interpretations of this message, and apply these to the context of our current life situation with its own unique problems and questions. This also requires serious study. One who has not gone through the complicated process of research and interpretation can easily come away from reading a passage of the Bible with a very wrong idea of what is being said. The words as they literally are presented can get in the way of the message just as easily as they can transmit the message, and people can easily read into God's word what they want to hear. History is filled with cases of people using Bible passages to justify engaging in the most antiChristian and barbaric of activities, even doing so in the name of religion.

Secondly, while all of Scripture is inspired and contains profound truth which is useful for teaching, not everything in the Bible is revelation about God. Sometimes what is revealed is not so much about God as it is about human beings. Sometimes a story is revealing the disastrous effects of human beings clinging to a false notion about God. A certain amount of training is required in order to be able to recognize these often subtle differences. This is the reason why in the past Catholics were warned against reading the Bible on their own. Today, however, with greater access to education for all, with the increased availability of research and study materials, and with the increasing number of reputable theological books about the Scriptures being published, Catholics are encouraged to read the Scriptures and reflect upon them, doing so in a rational and intelligent manner.

Thirdly, not everything written in the Bible is of equal importance. The reason that the Hebrew Bible, the Old Testament, is part of our Christian Scriptures is because it contains revealed information which is necessary in order to understand and appreciate what God has done in Jesus Christ. For a Christian to truly understand and fully appreciate the message of the Old Testament, it is necessary to know the New Testament. While the Hebrew Bible contains great depth, beauty, and truth in itself, a Catholic should read the New Testament first, and should always read the Old Testament in light of the message contained in the New Testament. One should then read the New Testament again, constantly referring to the Old Testament to appreciate even more fully the truth contained and developed in the New Testament. Above all, one should develop an appreciation for those aspects of Old Testament experience, which is really the experience of all of humanity in its search for God, that are corrected, superseded, or fulfilled by the answer to that search which is given in the person of Jesus.

Sacred Tradition

Scripture interpretation requires a shared common understanding, something against which we can compare the message we are seeing in order to gauge whether what we are seeing is on the right track. This is offered in our shared and living tradition, the second source of revelation for Catholics. God not only speaks to us in words, God also acts in and through human history, and especially through the history of the Church, his people. Jesus is God present as a part of human history, and Jesus remains with us throughout history until the end of time. Since Jesus reveals the Father, God's revelation is caught up with and expressed in and through human history as well. The very writing of Scripture followed this process. We see the unfolding knowledge of God grow and change in the Old Testament. We see Saint Paul draw out the deeper meaning of the Christ event for the people in response to their concrete problems and doubts, or the false understandings of Christ that were developing in the early Christian communities. As the Scriptures are themselves the beginning and the heart of our lived tradition, there is no clear line of demarcation or separation between Scripture and Tradition as sources of revelation. The two complement each other and are inseparable.

Tradition does not escape from the problem of interpretation. How do we discern whether what has happened is the will of God? How do we arrive at the knowledge of what God is doing behind what is happening? How do we answer the question raised about God's will by the death of a starving child or the destruction of a city by a tsunami? In part, we learn by trial and error, guided by the presence of the Holy Spirit. In our use of the sources of revelation we also make use of human reason. We do this by reasoning about and reflecting upon our experiences, personal and shared, and by dialoguing with other interpretations of other Christian religious perspectives. We look to our own lived experience and the shared wisdom passed on from generation to generation. We listen to other religions who are also searching for God and who all contain something of the truth about God. By joining the human tools of reason and science to the light of the truths revealed in the Scriptures and applying these to the study of historical events, the Church arrives at authoritative decisions about how to authentically interpret God's presence and activity around us. These decisions then enter into our living tradition and become part of the wealth of wisdom and knowledge which we can draw upon to interpret and recognize God's activity in the present and future. A theological principle which guides us in this process affirms that everything we need to know in order to be saved has already been revealed. There can be no new public revelation about God which alters, adds to, or contradicts what has already been revealed.

4. Theology Is a Coordinated Search for Faith's Understanding

As the study of theology became more and more professionalized, theologians began to specialize in one particular aspect of our faith experience. As we grow older as a Church, as we have more and more complex shared experiences to reflect upon, our living tradition continues to grow and is required to respond to new problems that didn't exist in earlier times. Dialogue with the tradition becomes more and more difficult to carry out on a global scale. There is just too much information to be effectively studied, processed, understood, and applied by any one person. Thus, faith in its search of understanding has brought about a number of different avenues, each of which centers in on one aspect of the faith experience itself, trying to unpack its meaning as fully as possible. Professional theology divides into branches in order to carry out its work more effectively. The main branches can be classified in many ways, but the relationship between them is easily seen if we link them by their particular area of study.

Theologies of Revelation Study the Sources and Content of Revelation

Scriptural theology scientifically studies the theological meaning and proper interpretation of the Scriptures. This study includes both scrutiny of the actual words of Scripture, as well as the background historical and cultural contexts necessary in order to identify and interpret the various levels of meaning contained in the words. Scriptural theology also attempts to distinguish those inspired passages of the Scriptures which are most revelatory.

Dogmatic theology studies our living tradition, in light of our tradition's understanding of Scripture, and attempts to identify and explain those basic beliefs, "dogmas," which identify us as members of a Church united by one faith. Belief in these dogmas unites us in faith, joins us together as a community of believers, and identifies us as members of the Catholic Church. This branch of theology also attempts to identify and understand those shared truths that are essential to salvation.

Christology studies the nature and meaning of Christ as savior. Christ is the definitive revelation of God to humanity. Christ is the second person of the Blessed Trinity become human in Jesus of Nazareth. Christ is one divine person with both human and divine natures. Thus he himself is the meeting point of both word and deed, Scripture and Tradition, humanity and divinity.

Ecclesiological Theologies Study the Nature, Meaning, and Vocation of the Catholic Church

Ecclesiology studies the nature of the Church itself as the body of Christ, the people of God, the privileged place where people come into contact with God in this world.

Sacramental theology studies the Church as a source of grace, and the seven ordinary means of grace instituted by Christ and given to the Church which bring salvation.

Liturgical theology studies our common activities of worship, the use and meaning of Christian symbol and ritual, the deeper meaning of what we do as a community of believers when we gather together to pray as God's people.

Soteriology studies the nature and effects of sin, the need for redemption, and the nature of the salvation that comes from Christ through the Church.

Practical Theologies Study the Way in Which We Effectively Live Our Faith

Pastoral theology studies the role of the Church's ministry in helping members of the Christian community live out the full meaning of their vocation as followers of Christ.

Moral theology studies what faith demands of us by way of lived response, so that we may come to appreciate how privileged we are to be called by Christ and how excellent this vocation is.

Ascetic or spiritual theology studies the processes of growth in holiness, the ways in which people can effectively focus mind and heart on loving and serving God alone, and the ways in which God calls and leads us into deeper relationship, especially through prayer.

These separate branches of theology are specialized investigations into particular questions which flow out of the main question that every Christian is required to ask: "What does it mean to believe?" As such, each of them must relate to the others as parts to the whole. Theology is one science. Dogmatic theology cannot be in conflict with scriptural theology. Moral theology and pastoral theology must be in harmony. Liturgical theology and sacramental theology must complement each other. When any one area of theological study is out of harmony with any other, this is cause for alarm and requires further questioning, investigation, and reformulation. The greatest challenge for theologians today as a result of their specialization is to constantly think about the ramifications of what they say within their own branch upon other areas. And as specialization increases, it becomes more and more difficult for a theologian working in one area to know what is being done in another. The current model for doing theology is an interdisciplinary one, with a number of specialists from different areas working together in order to discover the broader meaning of our shared religious experiences in and for the world today.

One of the primary functions of the official teaching magisterium of the Church is to ensure this harmony of all major areas of theological study. A theologian specializing in one area may not be familiar enough with the other areas, and he may fail to see that what makes sense within his own small enclosed field, when applied to other areas, doesn't fit into the whole. These types of tension and conflict are inevitable, and when these occur it can be cause for confusion within the theological world, and in the broader Church, precisely because the discipline of theology is at the service of all Christians who are theologians in the most basic sense.

5. Theology Is a Shared Search for an Understanding of the Faith

There are certain truths which do not and cannot change because they are grounded in God's activity and are so fundamental to what it means to be a follower of Christ that one cannot be called a Christian without believing in them. God exists. God is love. Christ is the Son of God. Christ through his life, death, and resurrection has set us free from the power of sin. There are also certain behaviors that one cannot indulge in regularly if one wants to call oneself a disciple of Christ. But the meaning that these truths have for us, the truths that are most important and useful to us at a given moment, and what knowledge of these truths demands from us in terms of concrete behavior, do change as we change and as our situations in life change. We never have the complete and total grasp either of these truths themselves or of their fullest meaning. We are not God. We are merely human beings seeking to know God, and we can never know God completely. No two persons experience Christ in exactly the same way. In sharing our experiences one with another we each learn from the other something about Christ we could not know otherwise. But we do this sharing within the broad framework of the basic and fundamental beliefs which we all share and which enable us all to make sense out of our personal and shared religious experiences.

The Sense of the Faithful

The search for understanding of what faith reveals as true continues and will need to continue throughout life and history. We Catholics believe that this search is guided by God's Holy Spirit as it dwells in the *Sensus Fidelium*, or the "common sense" of the believers. Our shared faith experience will not allow us as a Church to fall into any serious error concerning what we absolutely need to know. Were that to happen it would be the clearest sign that our faith was nothing more than invented knowledge of our own making. Furthermore we have the gift of the teaching magisterium of the Church, whose ministry it is to teach the wisdom contained in our Church's living tradition and to guide the faithful in their own personal theological task. Professional theologians aid the magisterium by providing it with the information it needs to fulfill its mission faithfully and by respectful critical analysis of what it teaches, so that it may express the truths of its teaching in more effective ways. And together they aid all followers of Jesus to make sense out of their daily faith experiences.

In the search for faith's meaning, we need not be afraid of disagreement. Tension is at the very heart of what historically has kept our living tradition alive. It is precisely the freedom to consider new ideas, new meanings, new applications of our shared faith traditions that enables the Church to respond effectively to life in our constantly changing world. The call of the Spirit is to unity of belief and practice. But unity should not be confused with strict uniformity. Unity in fact cannot attain its truest realization except when a healthy diversity of ways of understanding the meaning of the faith experience is present. Living with disagreements about meaning and making mistakes are not only the price we pay for our knowledge of the truth, they are the normal way in which we human beings arrive at knowledge of the truth. The history of our living tradition as a Church is full of bitter theological disagreements and terrible mistakes that were made. This is inevitable because we are a Church of human beings who argue about what they love and about what is important to them. What is important is to be able to recognize the difference between what is a mistake and what isn't, to learn from our mistakes so that we don't continue to repeat them, to use our arguing as a way of searching for deeper and more authentic understanding of our faith instead of falling into the childish trap of arguing about who is right, and to recognize that this process is both guided and protected by the presence of God's Holy Spirit.

The Magisterium

The Tradition of the Church usually contains many different theological understandings of the same faith reality. There rarely is just one possible explanation or understanding of religious experience or faith reality. It is the task of the magisterium, with the help of its professional theologians, to look into the tradition and to selectively teach those explanations or conclusions that will best serve the Church's faithful at this particular moment in history. As the social, political, economic, and daily life of people changes, what they need to know and understand about God, Christ, and the Church to help them live their daily lives also changes slightly. The teaching role of the Church is not just to proclaim the truth as if somehow saying the words magically solves every problem. The job is to proclaim the truth effectively, so that this truth can be heard by those who are in need of it, and in such a way that those who hear it are helped to understand it in a real, tangible, practical way. Church teaching itself develops and improves over time as the Church learns by living in this world the deep call to announce the good news its members need to hear.

The proper relationship of theologian to magisterium might be nicely illustrated by joining together two of the images used by Jesus in describing the kingdom of God. You do not pour new wine into old wineskins or you run the risk of losing both (Mark 2:22). New problems give rise to new questions and require new ways of understanding what faith reveals. But every wise head of a household knows how to take out of his storehouse both new and old (Matthew 13:52). It falls to the magisterium to teach our faith. To teach effectively, it must decide when to make use of new wineskins or older ones, what to take out of the storeroom of our tradition which is both new and old, and how to arrange them together. At times the magisterium needs theologians to inventory the storeroom and remind it of things that are there that might be useful, or suggest ways in which the old and new can be placed together side by side in very effective ways. At other times it might be necessary for the theologian to point out that putting new wine into old skins in the fashion being contemplated by the magisterium may cause both to burst. The magisterium also may at times need its theologians to be new wineskin makers. When the steward needs a new skin he doesn't make it himself. He goes to an expert on wineskins and then approves or disapproves of the final product. And in fact, most of the documents which communicate the official teaching of the magisterium of the Church are written by theologians. At times the magisterium might have to remind the theologian that neither the wine nor the wineskin belongs to him.

Theologians

This is fundamentally the healthy relationship of the magisterium to the theologian. When theologians teach theology in the name of the Church, they do so with the approval and with the authorization of the magisterium. They distribute the wine in the wineskins that were both approved by the steward. When they do theology as individual believers searching deeper understanding of their own faith, they do so as individuals. When acting as professional theologians fulfilling their responsibility of aiding the magisterium through critical analysis, they do so with other professionals in a professional forum of experts. It is important not to confuse these three functions and activities, although the theologian's personal challenge is to ensure that there is a coherence and harmony among all three of them. When able to accomplish this coherence, they fulfill their primary responsibility, which is to help the steward ensure that the best wine gets placed into the best possible wineskin, and is served in the finest goblets at the most well-designed table setting, so that the thirst of all of God's people can be adequately, and joyfully, quenched.

The Catholic Church has the benefit of having been here a long time and can apply the test Jesus himself has given us: by their fruits you shall know them. With more than two thousand years of lived experience the Church can safely say that if you live a certain way, the results will be disastrous; if you live a different way, you will find happiness; if you start believing that particular thing, it will lead you to contradiction and confusion; if you believe differently, it will lead you to deeper and more reasonable faith. We have seen this happen and our teaching is based on experience. This is why it is so necessary to have professional theologians in the Church today who are in contact with our Tradition and its theological sources. It enables us to remember what we as a Church have thought and done, and what did or did not lead us toward a deeper knowledge of the truth about God, life, ourselves, the meaning of Christ, etc.

The Individual Catholic

Faith cannot be content to let others outside of us decide its meaning for us. An external authority or teacher, even the magisterium, can share with us an official and shared understanding of faith. But that does not free us from the personal obligation to use our own power of reasoning to make that understanding our own. Just because the pope says something is true doesn't make it so. The pope teaches the truth, but he doesn't create or invent it. The individual Catholic has the obligation to listen very respectfully and to take very seriously the teaching of Church authority. But the obligation doesn't end there. We have to seriously think about this teaching and try to discover its truth for ourselves, making it part of our own understanding of the world and our place within it. We need to also read the theologians so that we can understand the official teachings of the Church more fully, where they came from, what they mean, why the Church is teaching what it is. The Holy Father can teach that life is sacred and must be respected from conception until death, that the wealthy have a moral obligation to use their wealth to help those in need, or any other concrete teaching but if individual Catholics do not take these teachings to heart, see and understand the truth contained in them, and make these a part of their daily living, the truth taught is mere words, without effect.

Theology's purpose is not to tell us what to think or what to do. Rather, theology is meant to guide us in our examination of what we really think, of how we are really living, and to help us in discerning whether our way of thinking and our way of living is that of Jesus Christ. If theology isn't helping us come to this deeper understanding of our faith which flows forward into life, it isn't theology. If we aren't searching to understand our faith more deeply, we aren't theologians. And if we aren't theologians, we really can't call ourselves true followers of Jesus Christ.

Chapter Two

Understanding the Fundamental Beliefs of the Faith Experience

The need to seek God is part of our own human nature. When we look seriously at ourselves, we soon see that in spite of our wonder and greatness, our ability to invent wonderful machines, to tame the skies and seas, to cure diseases, and to probe the mysteries of the universe and make sense out of them, there is still something fundamentally wrong with us. Despite our knowledge, our power, our good will, and our best intentions, we have not been able to learn how to live in peace with each other, to eradicate violence or hunger from our midst, to eliminate poverty and pain, or to activate our inner goodness. Saint Paul speaks about it quite powerfully in the seventh chapter of the Letter to the Romans. There is something inside of us that keeps us from doing what leads to the joy, happiness, and fulfillment that we seek, and which prevents us from enjoying fully the happiness that we have been able to attain. Saint Augustine said it a bit differently. Our hearts are restless. This lack of freedom over our own selves, this fear of being too content, too happy, too trustful of others, calls out for explanation. It reveals a deep hunger within us to be something more, greater, better than what we are. This universally shared human experience leads us to reflect and seek an answer to the question about what this means and why this is. If we are honest with ourselves, we come to realize that given the choices we have made, the stupid things that we have done in the past, and the opportunities that we have let pass by, we should not be in as good a condition as we are now. There has to have been someone or something watching over us and guiding and protecting us. Here we encounter the experience of something greater than ourselves, a mystery which calls out to us. We are led to seek an answer, a solution, and in this seeking we are gifted with knowledge of the Christ.

This thirst for an answer becomes even stronger if we turn our gaze toward the darker side of life. One does not have to be very old before hearing that famous phrase: "Life is not fair." Yet there is something which seems to be coded into our very genes that makes us rebel at the notion that life is not fair. We believe that there has to be a justice in the universe. Good people are not supposed to suffer for no reason. Bad people are supposed to be punished for the harm that they cause. But good people do suffer for no reason. Bad people apparently go merrily on their way, and even reap the rewards of their evil. Where is justice? Where is God?

Christian faith reveals that Jesus Christ is the Son of God become human, and that Jesus is not only the answer we are seeking, he is also the remedy for our situation. Hearing this, and experiencing ourselves as wanting to believe it certainly impels us to try to understand it. But before we can arrive at a deeper understanding of this truth which faith reveals, we first have to understand a few other things. Jesus as the answer is both God and human, and so we have to ask about what it means to be God, and about why people are the way we are. Then comes the question about why God chose to become human in the person of Jesus. And then, and only then, can we ask the real question on our minds, which is, what does all of this mean for me here and now in my life?

1. The Human Race—
The Glorious Image and Likeness of God

Delving into the Scriptures, at the very beginning of the Hebrew Bible in the first two chapters of the Book of Genesis, we find two different stories of the world's creation. The first story was written about nine hundred years before the birth of Christ, and the second story was composed about five hundred years later. These stories were never meant to be read as literal and historical descriptions of the creation of the world. The details of the two stories of creation actually contradict each other when they describe the creation of humankind. They don't in any way resolve the controversy about evolution or creationism which has become so heated and widespread in some religious circles. Rather than trying to tell us the specifics about how God created the world, each story attempts to communicate a unique truth about the relationship between God and humanity.

Reading these stories in light of Christ's teaching, we discover that God is first and foremost a creator. But God is also a trinity of persons existing in a relationship of unity. The three persons are sometimes referred to as the Creator, the Redeemer, and the Sanctifier, because we first come to know each by way of their activity. But the theological tradition has preferred to call them the Father, the Son, and the Holy Spirit, because these terms better express the relationship that joins each of the persons and reveals them to be much more than any or all of their actions. Each one always acts in union with the others, because the three persons exist in a relationship of oneness and love. We read of a loving creator, the Father, whose Holy Spirit hovers over the water of a formless void in darkness. Then, by the Father's speaking of a word (the *Logos*, or Son), light appears. In the light the formless void takes form. Order is brought out of the primeval chaos. Light is the fundamental prerequisite of vision. It makes photosynthesis possible, which produces the oxygen necessary for living beings to breathe, and so the presence of light on earth is needed in order for life to exist. Within this new order of light, the void becomes filled. Life bursts forth in ever greater abundance as time progresses. The crowning point of the process of growth and development in creation is achieved when God decides to make the human race in God's own image and likeness.

The Dignity of the Human Creature

These stories teach us a deep truth about what people are like and why. Unlike the other living creatures which God commands on the earth, in the sea, and in the air to bring forth,

God creates humanity directly. In one story we are made from nothingness. In the second story we are made from the mud of the earth, the most common and lowest of substances. But God directly breathes life into the new creature. It is God's own Spirit that brings us to life. From the beginning the human being is social. As humanity, as man and woman, we image God. Woman and man are meant to be equal and complementary. In the first story man and woman are created together at the same instant. In the second story the creature (Adam) has no gender until the moment when God creates the woman, taken from inside of Adam's body. Now he becomes man (*is*) at the moment that the woman (*'issah*) comes into being. His identity as man is defined by hers as woman and vice versa. The metaphorical progression is beautiful. Out of the void of nothingness comes something. Out of chaos comes order. Out of the order comes life. Out of life comes human life. Out of human life comes a relationship of love. All begins with God speaking the words, "Let there be Light", and ends with God breathing his own life (God's living Spirit) into the human race. And all of it is good. Human beings, like everything else in creation, are created to be good, have our place in nature, and are created for a purpose. The purpose of the human race, and our inherent goodness, is revealed in God's expressed intention—that we be God's image and likeness.

Being the image and likeness of God confers upon human beings a special dignity that no other creature in this world has. People are more precious and more necessary than any other created being in this world. Something of God is revealed in and through each and every human being.

Image and Likeness

A created object always bears the imprint of the one who created it. The real question here is, how exactly does humanity image God in its particular and unique way? There are many theological explanations in our tradition. Saint Irenaeus, one of the earliest theologians, thought of the "image" and the "likeness" of God as two separate realities. He defined the image of God as our physical human nature. All created beings image God in this way. There's nothing special here in humans. But Irenaeus saw the likeness of God as something special that only human beings have, which was given to us when God breathed his own life into the creature. The "likeness" enables the human being to see and to know God, and to live in conformity with God's will. Saint Augustine identified the image and likeness of God with immortality, which has its source in the soul. We discover what it means to image God by looking into our very humanity and touching that part of us which makes us human and distinguishes us from all other living beings. It is there in the soul of each person that God speaks to us and is revealed to us. Martin Luther identified the image and likeness of God as a relationship of original friendship or "righteousness" with God. Saint Thomas Aquinas interpreted the idea of the image of God in three related ways. There is a natural image of God, which all human beings have, that consists in having the ability to reason and to make free choices. The second way to image God appears when this natural ability to reason and choose is enlightened by God's grace in those who are baptized. A third way of imaging God is attained when this natural image that has been enlightened by grace is made perfect in the beatific vision, when we see God directly after death. A more contemporary approach sees the image and likeness of God in humanity as expressing the ongoing activity and presence of God in human history. Human creativity and social life images and expresses the underlying creative activity of God the Father. God's creative activity continues through humanity. God set creation in motion at the beginning of time and creation will continue to unfold and develop through human history until the end of time.

Today many theologians see the need to harmonize the central insights of our tradition about the image and likeness of God with what the sciences have discovered about the nature and origins of the human race. There is a renewed interest in going back to examine the wider tradition in an attempt to bring faith and reason together in a manner more in keeping with the discoveries of reason today. Some of the most promising results of this search are found in the theological movement called personalism. Many of the most important theologians of the past fifty years, including Karl Rahner, Bernard Häring, and Karol Wojtyla, have adopted this approach.

The Human Person

Personalism begins with the basic insight of Saint Thomas that human beings are persons. To be a person is to be an individual. To be a person is to be rational. To be a person is to be substantial. We are like God in our rationality, and in the fact that we each have our own individual and independent existence. We are persons in the same way that the three persons of the Blessed Trinity are persons, or that each of the angels is a person. But we are human persons, and so we image God as human persons in our own unique way. The unique fashion in which we image God as persons is contained in our human nature. When we look at human nature we see first of all that we are both matter and spirit in unity. We are body and soul joined together in oneness. We were not created by God to be pure spirits. We are meant to be body and soul joined together in inseparable unity. Secondly, our natures are rational and we are free. We do not act out of instinct. We have the power to reason and to choose.

Saint Thomas' limited notion of person is now developed and expanded to include other aspects which we have discovered about human nature during the past eight hundred years—things about human nature that Saint Thomas was not able to have known given the limitations of knowledge at the time he was writing. To the traditional notion that we image God as reasoning beings there have been added four other qualities essential to being a human person:

a) Human persons are subjects, and as subjects we are transcendent beings
b) Human persons are all fundamentally equal
c) Human persons are relational beings
d) Human persons create and share a common history and destiny

In addition to being rational and free, corporal and spiritual, human persons are also joined together in relationship, and we grow and change over time as both individuals, as groups, and as a human race. We define ourselves as subjects by our choices and actions, but at any given moment we are still more than what we have done or chosen. We have immense possibilities for future growth and change. We are more than the sum of our parts, the totality of our ideas. We are always reaching beyond for something more, greater, better. We are subjects who are seekers of God, but subjects who are related to other subjects in our search, seeking God together. We have a history which we create and share through our choices and actions, and this history also is meant to image God. We image God in our ability to relate to each other the way that the three persons of the Blessed Trinity relate to each other—in our power to love. We image God in showing mutual respect for each other, and in recognizing each other's dignity and equality. We image God in our ability to create a shared reality of history, culture, civilization, a social and personal order.

Here we touch the deeper meaning of these creation stories. Their basic point is that it is impossible to understand what it means to be human without making reference to God. To understand who and what we are, it is essential for us to seek to know God. Knowledge of God as three persons dwelling in oneness requires that we enter into relationship with each of these persons. In the beginning, God's created order was a paradise for people. The entire process of creation takes six days of actual work, culminating on the seventh day with God resting. Seven is a symbolic number which ex-presses perfection. The seven days of creation, rather than indicating seven actual days of twenty-four hours, is the author's way of saying that God's original creation was perfect. God and humanity dwell in harmony, and in a relationship of intimacy and friendship. The human beings know who and what they are because they are in constant contact with the God they image. Humanity and nature also are in harmony, both in our inner nature (with ourselves) and with external nature (our environment and other living creatures). People are happy, because by way of their relationship with God they know who they are, what they are, and why they are.

2. The Tragedy of the Fall into Sin

This perfect harmony is destroyed. The relationship of intimacy with God that reveals to them who they are is lost as the consequence of their own free choice. The story tells us of how the woman is tricked by a serpent to eat of a forbidden fruit, and she in turn convinces her husband to do so. It is important to understand the meaning conveyed by the details of the story. Why was the woman so easily tricked? Why did the man so easily accept the fruit that was offered? What exactly was the choice that was made? Who is responsible and what are the results?

We are told that the serpent is the most cunning of creatures. He appeals to two aspects of the innocent human being: naive trust in wisdom, and the very thirst for transcendence within human nature that makes us human. The woman is innocent, and the serpent makes use of his cunning and knowledge to corrupt and destroy that innocence, manipulating her very innocence to lead her into sin. Her sin is a sin of disobedience, but one brought about by naive belief in a lie

are not the direct punishment of an angry God. They are the natural consequences of the choice to look away from God. We read of God's anguish at seeing what they have done. God's words, rather than being an angry tirade, are words of sorrow. Without God they will know pain. Without God they will struggle. Without God they will die. The world is cursed because of them, but God does not curse them. Out of love God clothes them to hide their nakedness. But paradise is lost to them and to all of their descendants. The serpent however, does receive an angry curse from God and a severe punishment. God's anger is reserved for those who would use their knowledge and wisdom to corrupt and mislead the trusting and the innocent.

Here we come face to face with the core truths revealed in our faith tradition. Within the order created by our loving God, the human person holds a special place. Made in the likeness of God, the human person is different from all other animals or plants. The person is able to be a creator, as the God we image is a creator. Unfortunately, we do not always use the power of choice or the power of reason to create as God does. Rather than bringing order out of chaos, as God the creator does, we use our abilities to do the opposite. God is a relationship of loving persons: Father, Son, and Spirit all dwell in communion and community of love. Human persons are also relational beings. We are designed to find our happiness, our fulfillment only with and through relationship with other persons. But these relationships with others, in order to be successful and satisfying, must express knowledge of the way that Father, Son, and Holy Spirit dwell in relationship. When this knowledge is lacking, our relationships sour and transform into mechanisms of oppression, exploitation, and domination. Rather than using our relational power to join together in friendship, unity, and love, we often join together for the purpose of destruction of love, of other people's relationships and other people's lives. We become a living lie about God, a false image which no longer accurately reflects who God truly is.

3. The "Solidarity" of Human Slavery to Sin

The story is not just about our first parents. The history of Adam and Eve is the history of each and every human being. This fundamental flaw, which everyone sooner or later experiences, is what theologians call the state of original sin. It is an inescapable part of the inherited human condition. Human beings are not evil by our nature. We do however suffer from an inherited ignorance and weakness of will, and we are subject to powerful internal and external forces which affect our thoughts and desires. The desire to be something other than what we are created to be (to want to be God instead of being creatures who look to God to discover the meaning of our existence), brings pain and death, not only to those who sin in this way, but to other innocents as well. When instead of living to give glory and praise to God, we direct our efforts to bring glory and praise to ourselves, the consequences are always disastrous. Here is the result of giving into this desire, this dissatisfaction, this refusal to accept being what God has created and gifted us with being. We make use of our power of reason and choice to remake ourselves into something else.

We become cheap imitators of God rather than reliable images.

The Characteristics of Original Sin

We are taught and teach others to think in certain ways. We learn and cling to prejudices and fears. We see what we want to see, and we actively ignore realities that are unpleasant to us. We often easily mistake the truth for a lie and a lie for the truth. The flaw in our nature is inescapable and at times overwhelms us. This original sin is revealed in the powerful division we feel inside of ourselves between being a person as an individual, and a person who is part of a social group. We compete rather than cooperate. We want to be admired by others, yet we also see others as a threat. With the best of intentions, we often attempt to force uniformity rather than seeking to bring about unity, and this normally ends with one group imposing its views and opinions upon everyone. We demand that we be respected as persons, but often use others as objects for our own selfish purposes. We use the hallmarks of our human dignity, our reason and freedom, to decide that some of us are less than human and to treat them as such. We even hate in the name of love.

For a short period of time a few hundred years ago, during the period of history which theologians, historians, and philosophers call modernity, there was an overly optimistic belief that studying human nature scientifically would enable us to manipulate our social and personal lives in such a way as to cure all of these tendencies. This was a lofty endeavor, well intentioned and worthy of pursuit. However, it was a complete failure. We soon discovered that this new knowledge can also be and is used to serve the darker side of our nature as often as it is used to serve the lighter side. The period of the two world wars, and the brutal uses to which our knowledge of human social structures and psychology have been put to use by those in power to harm, exploit, and oppress others and to maintain their power or accomplish their purposes, have made us patently aware that science and knowledge are not able to save us from ourselves. We are still trapped in the disordered quality of our own human fallen state. And this is the fundamental insight of the story of the fall. We are fallen and we can't get up. Rather than living as the image of the true God, we transform our own lives into living idols of a false god created in our image, and this false god does not love us.

Two Views of Original Sin

Two main theological approaches try to make sense out of this truth about ourselves. The first holds that our natural and original perfection was either lost or severely damaged as the result of sin's entry into human history. Our minds are now dimmer than they should be. Our wills are weakened. Sin takes us over, gaining a power over human beings and our history. We require redemption, and a salvation flowing out of redemption which will restore what was lost. This theological current became very powerful in Catholic tradition. We need a savior to destroy the power of sin over us and repair the damage that was done to our human nature and restore to us what was lost. The savior will enable us to once again know the God in whose image we are created. An alternative approach offers an evolutionary or developmental explanation. Instead of seeing the weakness or imperfection of people as the result of having lost something that was originally present, original sin is presented as the natural consequence of immaturity and incompleteness. God's creation of humanity is still underway and is not yet finished. People are still not what they are meant to be in God's mind, because God hasn't yet finished with them. We still do not understand who God is and what being the image of God means because we haven't yet developed the ability to understand. As history unfolds, God makes use of our shared history to reveal himself to us, to teach us, to bring us growth, and to move us forward in the development of our God consciousness. In this view, Christ is the perfect model of what we are all meant to one day become. But he is much more than that. He is the way to become God's image, the definitive force which makes it possible for us to make a great leap forward and through whom the ongoing creation by God the Father is brought to its completion.

Regardless of which of these explanations seems more satisfying, the actual details of how this state of original sin entered into history are not as important as what its presence means for us. The Catholic Church tradition defends the fundamental message contained in the scriptural story. This is not God's fault, nor was it ever God's intention for us to be this way. It is God's will that the human person know happiness. This bears repeating, since it is easily forgotten. Given the amount of suffering which is so present in the world today, it is easy to fall prey to the false notion that somehow or other this is God's will; that God either delights in or wants our suffering. It is the Christian understanding that God wants us to be happy, and God makes it possible for us to be happy. Suffering is the consequence of our own choices, not God's. It is the enduring effect of sin. There is something missing in our nature that is supposed to be there. And when we reflect theologically on this story we should come face to face with a serious truth about ourselves. We each carry within us this same weakness which leads us to personally sin. When we freely and deliberately choose to act upon it, we harm ourselves, add to the chaos of the world, damage our relationship with God and with other people, and increase the power of sin. Saint Paul refers to this as being slaves. Pope John Paul II called it participating in the creation of a culture of death. But the meaning is the same. The more we give in to it, the more this flaw takes us over, until we find ourselves incapable of resisting.

The Essence of Sin

The term sin in our Catholic tradition has many different meanings. It is a moral infraction, the breaking of a commandment, and an offense against God. But the most basic of all meanings of sin is that which we find in the Scriptures themselves. The word used is *hamartia*, which literally means "missing the target." This is the essence of sin. It is missing the point of life; not living up to what we were created to be. When sin is understood in this sense, the other meanings become clearer. If we can't see God, we don't even know what the target is. The commandment is a visible marker which points out to us the target. Behind the negative formulation "thou shalt not kill" is the positive statement that we are to love, respect, and value life. Behind the statement "thou shalt not commit adultery" is the positive statement about how honoring fidelity and marriage can lead us to fulfillment and happiness. This also explains how sin is offensive to God. Our personal sin robs us of the ability to attain the happiness that God has desired for us since the beginning of creation. This is what is offensive to God. Our sin harms the people that God loves. We do not appreciate or live in harmony with the goodness of what God has created, or we actively mar or destroy that goodness, or we try to put something else of our own creation in its place. All sin is fundamentally a rejection of our own humanity. All sin is fundamentally an idolatry. All personal sin flows out of and flows back into this original turning away from God as source and center of our human existence.

The Effects of Sin

If being a person were merely an individual reality, one's sin would be his or hers alone to bear. But that is not how human persons are built. We are persons in relationship with other persons. We define our very identity as individuals by making reference to the groups to which we belong. And so our individual sin always has an impact upon others. My actions do not only affect me. They affect others as well. They have an impact on how others see and relate to me, and often others are directly harmed as a result of my misuse of reason and will. Often the effects of our inhuman activity continue for generations, as the effects of one action are causes of other actions. Cycles of vengeance and family feuds are powerful examples of how sin breeds its own future. Children born into a family warring with another are taught from birth to hold a grudge for what was done long before they were born. The parents eat sour grapes and their children's teeth are set on edge (Jeremiah 31:30). We create social and economic structures which turn against us and begin to control us. The realities of racism, the uncritical patriotism or religiosity which leads us to look down on persons of other religions or countries or cultures as inferior, the prejudices and fears that divide us even from others within our own cities and countries, all give testimony to the power of sinful solidarity over our minds and our wills. Even when we know that these things are wrong, we often find it nearly impossible to resist their power over us. Sin blinds our reason and weakens our wills, not just as individuals, but as groups, as nations, as Church, and as a human race.

This misuse of freedom and knowledge leads to its complete perversion. In the name of freedom we actually turn ourselves into slaves. We gradually begin to confuse lies with truth and truth with lies. And this is exactly what we see in the entire Old Testament theological history of humanity. It is the history of sin building upon sin and God's constant interventions in human history to make things right. What begins as one small sin multiplies and grows until knowledge of God's original plan for humanity is perverted and lost.

But our God is a God of love, who does not abandon us to our own self-destructive ignorance. God constantly intervenes in human history in many different ways, calling individuals and using them to draw together a group of people so that he can make himself known to them. God calls Abraham to make him the father of a great nation. God calls Moses to set the people free from slavery in Egypt, and leads them through the desert to form them into a people joined to God in a covenant relationship. The constant activity of God shows concern for the individual as a member of a community. God speaks to the people through prophets, making his will known and instructing the people by giving them laws and commandments. It is the principal role of both the law and the prophet to remind them of who they are as a people, of what it means to image and glorify God as a people. But even those who know the one God are unable to liberate themselves from their own misdirected use of free choice. They are unable to keep the laws, understand the teachings and what they require, or to follow the commandments. Each new act of turning away, of idolatry, sinks all of fallen humanity more deeply into the quagmire of its own sin. Humanity without a clear vision of God becomes a people walking in the darkness of their own creation.

God then intervenes definitively to put things right. The intervention however does not come from outside of humanity with God sticking a hand in as an outsider. The resolution of the sinful solidarity of humanity by a loving God comes from within humanity itself, in the person of Jesus Christ.

4. The Christ Event— God's Answer to Human Sin

The meaning of Jesus' life is summarized in the prologue to the Gospel of John, which brings our thoughts back to God's original intention for the human race. In the beginning was the Word (*Logos*). This Word is that same living word spoken by the Creator which brought order out of the primeval chaos.

The Word of light spoken is the second person of the Blessed Trinity—the Son of the Father. We are told that it is through him that all things that came to be. The Word has become human flesh and blood in Jesus, and has lived among us. He is the divine light returned to the world so that we will again be able to see, and through whom God the Father will again breathe into us the divine spirit of life. In his own words, the living light tells us why he has come: God did not send the son into the world to condemn the world, but that the world might be saved through him (John 3:17). The mission is one of restoration and reconciliation. His purpose is to bring people back into a relationship of love and intimacy with the Creator. He is going to undo the damage brought about by sin. How he accomplishes this reconciliation between God and humanity is contained in the very details of his life and ministry as we read them in the New Testament. Unlike the first parents, who brought chaos back into the world through prideful disobedience, he as the new representative of the human race will restore us to our original dignity through humility and obedience to the Father's will. But he is also the perfect image of the Father, who will reveal to us exactly what it means to be the image and likeness of God. Thus he is the way to the Father, he is the truth about the Father, he is the key to understanding the meaning of human life.

The events surrounding Christ's coming, in addition to being a wonderful story, are themselves revelatory. In the beginning, both man and woman were involved in the fall, and both made ill use of their reason and will. Now in the coming of the Son of God, a man and a woman will cooperate in making proper use of their freedom to choose. Eve, after her sin, became the mother of all the living, and original sin passed from one generation to the next. Now a new Eve will be given, specially prepared to be the mother of a new Adam who will reverse and restore what had been damaged and lost. The new Eve will become the mother of all those living in the new creation.

God specially prepares Mary, the mother of Jesus, by allowing her to be conceived without original sin, a truth of faith which we Catholics call the "Immaculate Conception," so that she can be a fitting and worthy receptacle for his son, soon to become incarnate. An angel announces to her that she has been chosen to be the mother of the Redeemer. But she still has a choice. Unlike the first mother, whose choice was to try to become equal to God, the Virgin Mary responds as both creature and saint with the words, "Here am I, the servant of the Lord; let it be with me according to your word" (Luke 1:38). Thus Jesus is miraculously conceived in her womb. Her life will now be defined by her free choice to accept the Word made flesh. It is for this reason that Mary holds such a special place of honor among Catholics. She will become the perfect model for all Christians of what it means to be saved. It is precisely her humanity that makes her so special to us. She is what we are all enabled to be by Christ. She is what we are called to become. Christ comes into the world through her. She bears him inside of her and gives him to the world. She dedicates her life to doing the will of God.

Joseph, the man she had been betrothed to marry, must also make an act of faith. His is not only an act of faith in God, but also of faith in her. The woman he loves is pregnant, and he is not the father. She tells him of a vision, of an angel, of a virginal conception. And it is not until he himself shares the vision that he is able to see what she has seen. He is given the gift of the vision of faith, and this vision not only allows him to put his faith in God, but also to put his faith in his wife, in another human being joined to him in love. He learns and teaches us the important lesson that even love is impossible unless faith is present. Faith in God makes faith in those we love more possible, and if we lose faith in each other, our ability to accomplish God's will is lessened. But faith in the persons we love also becomes a source of our faith in God.

The Redemptive Kenosis

Mary gives birth to Jesus in poverty. We read in Matthew's Gospel that there is no place for them. John reminds us that he came to his own, and his own did not receive him. The light came into the world, and people preferred darkness. These aspects of the Christ story illustrate a deeper reality at work, which theologians call the divine *kenosis*. *Kenosis* is a Greek word which means "emptying" or "condescension." Saint Paul writes eloquently about it in the second chapter of his Letter to the Philippians, reminding us that the second person of the Blessed Trinity, the Word, is and was from the beginning of time, God. He had everything. He was everything. Yet the Son did not cling to equality with the Father and the Spirit. Rather he emptied himself of his power and his glory, and became human, taking upon himself the condition of a slave (that of fallen humanity enslaved by the power of sin). Unlike the first Adam who rejected his humanity and aspired to be equal to God, the new Adam in Jesus will lay aside his equality with God and embrace humanity. Paul even goes so far as to say that he who was without sin became sin for us (2 Corinthians 5:21).

This does not mean that Jesus sinned, but that Jesus will freely choose to suffer in his life the consequences of the sin of others. He will be born into poverty. He will be used by those who seek him out and show him friendship only because of what he can do for them. He will suffer the effects of reprisal at the hands of those who become jealous of him, or see him as a threat. He will be falsely accused of doing the good that he does for a hidden and duplicitous motivation, even to the point of accusing him of being in league with Satan, of being possessed by an evil spirit, of being crazy. The people he is closest to in his life will misunderstand him, even betray him. He will be falsely accused and suffer torture at the hands of people who believe that they are doing the will of God. Eventually he will receive a death sentence for the sake of political expediency and be legally executed even though he is innocent. People will enjoy watching him suffer, will laugh at him as he dies. For one brief moment just before his death, he will experience the very heart of the state of human sin as he feels completely cut off from his father, crying out in anguish, "Why have you forsaken me?" All of these terrible events are the results of other people's human blindness and bad choices that Christ voluntarily chooses to endure. Christ becomes a living example of what sin does to people. Too often in life, the innocent pay the price in pain of the sins of the guilty. If one wants to stare the dark side of human life and sin directly in the face, and see the horror of what we are capable of doing and becoming, all we need do is look on the face of Christ crucified.

It was not God the Father who demanded that Jesus die in this way. From the moment of his becoming human, acceptance of his humanity would require dying. To be human is to eventually face death, and Jesus was and continues to be fully human. Resurrection and triumph over death is impossible unless one dies. But the manner and moment of Jesus' death was chosen by people. The choice of his death, and the glee experienced by those who demanded it, reveal how blind, weak, and evil humanity had become. His persecution, torture, and murder was done in the very name of God. In the cross of Jesus we see not only the source of our redemption, but also the need we have for that redemption. Christ willingly submits to the hate, the violence, the death, not in a passive or morbid or codependent manner, but actively, consciously, and deliberately in order to absorb the evil into his own goodness and transform it into life again. He conquers darkness with light, evil with goodness, sin with forgiveness, hatred with mercy.

The Cross

This is the reason why Catholics are so given to place the crucifix in our homes, to wear it around our necks, to make the sign of the cross on entering and leaving Church. The cross of Christ for us is not a symbol of suffering, pain, death, and misery, but a symbol of hope and victory. Christ has triumphed over the power of sin. While being tortured and rejected by those he came to serve and save, he resisted the temptation to hate, to seek vengeance, to call down legions of angels to destroy. Instead, he imaged the Father, who out of love understands and forgives. In accepting death on the cross rather than bringing death in anger, or fear, or vengeance, he reveals the depth of spirit and the greatness that human beings created in the likeness of God are capable.

The cross transmits a powerful message which sustains us in times of difficulty. On the cross Jesus experienced a loss of vision of the presence of the Father. He was in darkness, crying out in anguish as he sought comfort from his God and found none. In the emptiness though, Christ was still able to make an act of faith, commending his spirit into the hands of his, to all appearances absent, Father. In spite of the fact that the Father could not be seen, felt, or heard, even by Jesus himself, the Father was there to receive his Spirit, and three days later raised his fallen Son to glorified life. Here on the cross is revealed the true depth and mystery of faith. God is present even when we cannot feel his presence. Even when there are no tangible signs that God is here, God never abandons or leaves us. At those times when the darkness is darkest (and the crucifixion of Christ was as dark as darkness gets), when evil appears to be winning, we can be sure that the good will endure and ultimately triumph, because in the resurrection Christ has conquered the power of darkness. The lack is in our ability to see, not in the Father's lack of presence or love. What blindness there remains is in our eyes, not in the lack of light shining in this world. This is what gives us hope. When we look on the face of Christ crucified and think of our own trials and sorrows, we are reminded that no matter how alone we might feel, we are not alone. No matter how often we fail, God will make things right. No matter how much death is all around us, resurrection will follow. The Father is there waiting to transform our fear into courage, our pain into joy, our suffering into redemptive power, our death into life. When we look upon the face of Christ crucified and think of the trials and sorrows of others, we know what it is that we are called to do. We see clearly that we are sent by Christ to be his living message of comfort, hope, and help to them.

The Power and Meaning of the Incarnation

This *kenosis* of Jesus has two principal effects. In the person of Jesus, God himself experiences the weakness of our human nature personally and directly. God experiences empathy with our fallen condition. Secondly, there arises a solidarity of action which flows out of this empathy. The Jesus that feels the pain of those who suffer relieves that pain and shows people how their own bad choices and lack of understanding of the truth have been the causes of that pain. But he does not naively preach that all people's pain is their own fault. Instead, the message is one of the recognition of solidarity and the existence of structures of sin and their power over human life. He offers a teaching which can resolve the problem—that of solidarity in action. Rather than fixing the blame for one's suffering, we are called to join together first of all to relieve the pain, and once the pain has been eased, to eliminate the causes that gave rise to it. Above all we are called to forgive. At times doing this requires taking the pain, or a portion thereof, upon ourselves. It requires sacrifice. At other times it requires accepting responsibility for our part in having been part of its cause and making reparations.

Here again the face of original sin rears its ugly head. It has been demonstrated quite convincingly by psychology that if we are able to convince ourselves that someone's suffering is his or her own fault, we find it difficult to empathize, to feel sympathy. The normal response may even be one of satisfaction or pleasure in seeing that they are getting their "just desserts." Often it is only when we become convinced that someone in pain is unjustly suffering as an innocent at the hands of another that we are willing to come to their aid. A person dying of AIDS caused by a life of promiscuous behavior often receives less attention, sympathy, even physical care than a person who has been infected in an emergency blood transfusion. The perception is that the first deserves what he is getting, and the other has been harmed. It's just one very short step to make use of this distinction in order to justify ignoring those who suffer or to even rationalize adding to their suffering. We are also able to use our gift of reason to find reasons to justify what we want, even when those invented reasons are lies.

This is the key to understanding Jesus. He is God who has become a servant in service to humanity. When we read the story of the life of Jesus contained in the gospels, we see a gradual process of continual emptying. Christ does not come to do his own will. He comes to do the will of the Father. And he constantly reminds us that the Father does not think the way that human beings do. He does not selfishly hold on to what is his. He freely gives and teaches others to do so. The *kenosis* continues and reaches its most eloquent final completion as he even empties his very body of its blood on the cross. He "pours out" his life so that others may have life in greater abundance. The way that he serves is defined by what he says and what he does. Since his life work is to do the will of his heavenly Father, we come to a knowledge of the will of the Father by looking at what he does with and for others and by listening to his teachings. If we wish to know what it means to be the image and likeness of the true God, and how to properly be the image of God that we were created to be, all we need do is look at Jesus.

The very first lines of the Letter to the Hebrews reminds us that in the past God spoke in many but ambiguous ways, but that in our lifetime God has spoken clearly in his Son. Jesus will tell his apostles that those who have seen him have seen the Father. What do we see when we look at Jesus? First and foremost he reminds humanity of its original dignity. What is done to the least of our brothers and sisters is done to him (Matthew 25:31-46). The way we treat others is the way we respond to God. People are the image and likeness of God, and the first and most important place where we human beings encounter God. Forgiveness and healing become the two hallmarks of the ministry of Jesus. He heals the sick. He casts out demons. He raises the dead. He forgives sin. He shows compassion, even for the guilty. He shows special care and attention to those whom society has stigmatized, rejected, abandoned. He has harsh words for only one group of people: the self-righteous, those who think that they are better than others and who feel justified in judging and looking down on others in their weakness; those who point out and condemn other people's weakness and sin in order to mask their own; those who bind up heavy loads to place on other people's shoulders but will not lift a finger to lighten the load; those who teach as divine commandments the laws of their own invention.

Divinization

Jesus told us that the Son of Man came to seek out and save that which was lost (Luke 19:10). Another way of saying this is the famous affirmation of Saint Athanasius that God became man so that man could become God. In modern language this sounds almost blasphemous, but the phrase expresses a deep truth about the meaning of the incarnation of the Son of God in Jesus Christ. The second person of the Blessed Trinity has become fully human in order to restore to us our original dignity as the image and likeness of God. Saint Gregory of Nazianzus reminded us that in order to accomplish this, Christ had to unite himself fully to human nature. That which has not been assumed has not been redeemed. And the fourth chapter of the Letter to the Hebrews reminds us that we have a high priest who was tempted in every way we are. Jesus was fully human. He was also fully divine. The Word became human, living flesh and blood in inseparable union.

In the person of the risen Jesus, both humanity and divinity are joined forever. This means that we look to Jesus in order to understand what we were created to be. He is the perfect model for those who are redeemed and saved. If the human person's original destiny is to be the image of God in this material world, then looking at the person of Jesus we see the perfect image of the Father in human flesh and blood. If we want to know God's intention for us, and what we are now called to become, we need look no further than the person of Jesus Christ. He teaches us by word and example what being the image and likeness of God in this world means. But more than this, by the power of his death and resurrection in obedience to his Father's will, Christ has made it possible for us to actually live the likeness of God which has been imprinted into each of us. In the resurrection of Jesus' body in its glorified state, fallen humanity is now resurrected forever. Life is eternal not only for the soul, but for the body as well. We were created to be body and soul, matter and spirit joined in inseparable unity. Redemption is only complete when body and soul are joined in immortality. This is why the resurrection becomes the focal point of our life of faith as Christians. What form the body will take in resurrected eternal life is not known to us. But whatever form it will take we can have a foretaste of here on this earth. By joining ourselves in unity to Christ in and through his Church, our heaven begins here and now in our experience of the power that flows out of our union with the Lord.

The Risen Christ and the Church

The life and ministry of Jesus is circumscribed by three major roles. Jesus is a priest. Jesus is a prophet. Jesus is a king. Jesus is the fulfillment of the Law and the Prophets, and so his role as prophet and king can only really be understood as the extension of his priesthood. As priest his job is to sanctify, to make humanity holy. He offers his very life in sacrifice to the Father in atonement for the sins of fallen humanity. He shatters the power of sin over our lives. The greatest sacrifice is that of the *kenosis* itself brought to completion on the cross and carried on in the sacrament of the Eucharist. As prophet his task is to teach, to speak the word of God to people. Jesus is himself the Word of God made flesh, and his very life speaks the will of the Father. His teachings are recorded and continue to speak to us in the Scriptures, especially in the gospels. As king his task is to govern, to give laws for living in the kingdom of God his Father. In fulfillment of his kingly role he gathers apostles and disciples together and joins them to his body in the covenant of communion, sending them out to proclaim the good news of salvation and make believers of all nations. He gives them a new set of commandments which summarize and complete the older law: that they love each other. He forms them into the Church, and he promises to remain with them until the end of time.

These three ministries which define Christ are joined into one, as the risen Jesus brings the Church into being. He bestows upon his followers the power to forgive sin and commands them to do so. Jesus orders them to carry on his saving activity until he returns. He makes of them the way that he will continue to draw all people to himself until the end of time. Christ sends his Holy Spirit upon the apostles on Pentecost, giving them both courage and power to teach effectively, govern wisely, and sanctify efficaciously all those who become joined to the Lord in communion of heart and mind. The Holy Spirit remains with the Church until the end of time. The Spirit reveals God's will through Scripture and Tradition, forges the Church into a historical and hierarchical institution, and guides the Church in its task of authentically interpreting revelation. The Spirit transforms the Church into a new civilization of redeemed and sanctified human persons. This new "people of God," is the restoration of the relationship between God and humanity. It is the place where the risen Christ continues to dwell among us. In the reality of the Church, his is the right of sovereignty over the earth. Those of us who believe in him and are members of his body not only owe all loyalty to him and him alone, but we also share in his kingship. This is our Father's world and our inheritance, and we as the Church are God's stewards.

The Reign of God

As a result of the life, death, and resurrection of Jesus Christ there is no longer any barrier between heaven and earth. Heaven has come to earth and earth is raised to heaven. Rather than living in this world in order to escape it and get into the next, our task is to express and reveal the unity between this world and the next by the way we live our lives. Our call as a Catholic Church is to build the kingdom of God. Our heaven begins here and now. Eternal life is present already for those redeemed in Christ. As Jesus himself reminds us, eternal life is knowledge of the one true God and Jesus Christ whom he has sent (John 17:3). Heaven is merely the continuation of what we are already living and experiencing here. Once one has the experience of eternal life, there is nothing left to fear. This is powerfully symbolized in Matthew's Gospel account of the crucifixion. As Christ breathes his last breath, the veil of the temple is torn from top to bottom. The veil symbolizes the inability of people to know God or to come into the presence of God. It is the veil which separates the world of spirit and matter, of earth and heaven. The earth trembles and gives up its dead. Heaven and earth are now joined. Sin and its power that leads to death have been defeated.

The cross and resurrection of Christ define our identity as the Catholic Church. The vertical beam of the cross joins heaven and earth, reminding us that this life and the next are joined in continuity. We cannot make sense of our daily activities here on earth unless we relate them to what lies beyond this world. The temporal is joined to the eternal. What we do here has consequences that go far beyond this moment, this action, this situation. The horizontal beam of the cross which holds the outstretched arms of Jesus embraces all of this world, all of humanity, and reminds us that the Lord continues to yearn to draw all people to himself. It is our call and mission to bring those in need of Christ's gift to him, and it is a reminder that we as a human race are all brothers and sisters, children of the one Father. It is the clearest symbol of what we are as the Catholic Church and of the work which still remains to be done. Christianity is the first and most authentic humanism, precisely because the incarnation of Jesus Christ reminds us that our very humanity cannot be understood, appreciated, or authentically lived without reference to God, and that our relationship to God depends upon the way we relate and respond to our fellow human persons who are God's image in this world.

This vision of faith enables us to see the pettiness of our group loyalties, our selfish squabbles, and inspires us to open our hearts to our brothers and sisters in need, making their sufferings our sufferings, and joining our lives to the continuing caring and healing work of Jesus which remains alive and active in his Church. At the meeting point of vertical and horizontal beams is the face of the Lord. He is the point where heaven and earth are one, and where I and all other people are brought into oneness of heart, mind, and spirit. The blood which pours from his hands, feet, and side, running down the cross and staining the earth reminds us that Christ has transformed this world into his altar. It is the place where God becomes present to his people. This world is sanctified by his blood. This world is holy. And so the Church must be a prophet to this world, reminding it of what Christ has done here and how Christ has transformed it.

This is what we see when we look on Christ crucified. It is the message we are called to prophetically proclaim. The crucifix is not a symbol of a passive god who teaches us to allow others to hurt us, or of an angry God waiting to do to us what was done to his Son. It reveals a loving God who goes to these extremes to communicate love to us. Ours is a God who readily forgives the unforgivable, who suffers to alleviate and remedy the suffering that we cause to ourselves by our own selfishness and stupidity, and who enables us to do the same for each other. The Christ event does not end with the cross. It continues. Jesus is raised from death and walks among us. Resurrection is the restoration of eternal life, and eternal life is found in the risen body of Jesus. The risen body of Jesus continues to be present in this world and we experience this presence by way of the Church. This is what gives us hope, courage, and strength to endure, and this is what draws us into deep communion with each other as his disciples.

The story of our redemption doesn't end with the death and resurrection of Jesus. The story continues in the Church. The Spirit of God descends upon the apostles and sends them throughout the world proclaiming the good news of salvation. In the experiences and teachings of the apostles and martyrs, we continue to see how the power of Christ continues to bring life out of death, growth out of suffering, hope out of despair, until the word of God arrives in Rome, and from there begins to fan out to fill the world. To this very day, in its missionary and social ministry, the Catholic Church continues to be the place where Christ is lifted up and draws all people to himself, and where we discover what it means to be truly and fully the image and likeness of God that we are created to be.

Chapter Three

Living the Christian Mystery—The Nature and Reality of Salvation

Salvation comes through Christ by way of the Church. Christ wants to save every human being. Salvation is a free gift. But what is salvation? Salvation is not getting into heaven after you die. Heaven is our eternal reward, the fulfillment of a life of fidelity. Salvation is never a reward. It is not something that we can earn, deserve, or buy. It is something we desperately need. Neither is salvation having your sins forgiven. That is justification, or reconciliation, the restoration of a relationship with God. Salvation is not having had the price of our sins paid for with the blood of Christ. That is redemption, which restores our status as children of the Father and makes salvation possible. All of these realities are essential parts of the Christ event and related to salvation.

1. Christ Saves Us

Salvation is a practical reality which orients our life to God and makes it possible to live our lives in a truly Christian way. Salvation is not something we get. It is an action of God which becomes active in us. Salvation is freedom from the power of original sin and the healing of the ongoing effects of original sin. Salvation enables us to do what is good and to reject what is evil. In Catholic theology, salvation means that I have received in this given moment, in this concrete situation, the power to see the good as God wills it, and the strength of will to do whatever is necessary and possible to realize that good. I have been given the clarity of vision to see the evil that tempts me, and I have received the strength of will to resist that evil, no matter how great the cost of doing so. This is the gift of being able to live authentically as the image and likeness of the true God. It is also the gift which inspires us to want what God wills for us. A lifetime of fidelity in living out the gift of salvation will culminate in an eternity of union with God, but salvation is about life here and now. The theological way of saying this in the Catholic tradition is that the salvation which comes to us in Christ is "efficacious." Salvation changes us and makes a real difference in this world and in our daily lives.

2. Christ Graces Us with Salvation

Salvation is the result of grace. It is tempting to think of grace as if it were a thing, like a bottle of medicine or spiritual money. But grace is not a thing. Grace begins with an action on the part of God. It is the manifestation of God's love in the person of Jesus Christ. Grace is an experience of this love of God in our lives that strengthens the spirit, enlightens the mind, and strengthens the will. Grace is the natural consequence of having found God within our lives. The more we experience God's grace, the better we recognize the presence and action of God all around us. Grace grows and feeds upon its own power to transform us and mold us into the image and likeness of the true God that is revealed to us in Christ. God is everywhere and involved in everything, and so grace can happen at any time and anywhere. Every single moment is an opportunity for grace. Every human person is an opportunity for grace. A true appreciation of the gift of God's grace requires learning to look, to recognize, to see God present and at work all around us. Our relationship with Christ the Light makes this vision of God's presence possible.

Theology distinguishes between two types of grace on the basis of our experience of what each does for us, but there is no real line of separation between them. Grace is grace. There is sanctifying grace, which is experienced as a direct personal loving relationship with God. By way of sanctifying grace we enter into a personal relationship with Jesus Christ. Jesus is the Son of the Father dwelling in a relationship of love with the Father and the Spirit. Through our personal relationship of love with Christ we are drawn into the very life and love of the Divine Trinity. Sanctifying grace makes us holy, consecrates us, and is the true source of salvation. There are also other graces, called actual graces, which flow out of sanctifying grace as its effects. These secondary graces provide us with the ability to activate sanctifying grace in specific situations. They enable us to see what is hidden, to recognize what needs to be done in order to live the meaning of our sanctifying grace, and to deepen our relationship with God.

Saint Thomas Aquinas taught the theological principle that "grace builds upon nature." God saves us precisely as human persons. God works from within and through our own fallen humanity by raising it, transforming and sanctifying us. This is the whole message and meaning of the Christ event. We are by our nature a unity of body and soul, reasoning and free individual personal subjects joined in relationship with others who, together, create a common shared history and future. Grace works in and through these aspects of our human nature. A nourishing meal given to a hungry person, a family celebration which strengthens the joy of loving, the discovery of a new medicine able to alleviate suffering or cure a serious illness, all can become concrete ways in which God's grace appears. The grace of God strengthens and heals the flagging spirit, the failing body, the broken relationships. It takes the will that has been weakened, the mind and the conscience that have been blinded as the result of personal and shared sin, and strengthens and enlightens these.

3. Christ Graces Us Through the Church

The sacraments are the ordinary ways in which Christ graces people through his Church. Sacraments are defined as visible signs instituted by Christ to give grace. The Catholic Church teaches that the sacraments confer grace upon people *ex opere operato,* which means that the sacrament's effectiveness comes from God's loving action and doesn't depend upon the quality of either the minister or the recipient. One does not have to be perfect for grace to be given or received. If a person receives the sacrament, that person receives the gift of grace, as long as no obstacle has been placed in the way. In our early catechesis we memorize the names of the sacraments and a phrase or two about what each does. That is sufficient knowledge for a child. But for the sacraments to really attain their full power in our lives as adults, our knowledge has to go far deeper than what we were taught as children. If we want to reap the fullest benefit of the sacraments, it helps to understand what God is doing for us through the sacraments. We should really participate in them intentionally, and want them to accomplish what they are designed by Christ to do for us. God doesn't force gifts upon us. The gift must be freely accepted and embraced. Knowledge of what we are being given makes this easier and also fosters in us an attitude of gratitude. So it becomes very important for us as adult Catholics to understand the meaning and the power of the gifts that the sacraments are.

The Church Is the Place of Encounter with God in Christ

In Catholic tradition there are seven sacraments. All seven flow out of and are functional expressions of the one deeper sacrament, the Church. We are talking here about the Church in its broadest sense as the community of all those on earth who are in union with Christ. The Church is often called the *ur*, or primordial sacrament. It is the foundational or first sacrament, because it was instituted by Christ for the purpose of carrying on his saving work. The Church is the privileged place where we encounter the love of Christ most powerfully, and it is the place where one has access to the other sacraments. Each of the seven sacraments is one concrete way in which the Church carries out its fundamental mission. God wants all people to be saved. Salvation comes through Christ. Christ comes to us through the Church. The main purpose for the existence of the Church is to bring people into relationship with Christ. The seven sacraments are the ordinary and also the most powerful means by which the Church fulfills this purpose. The sacraments bring us into personal contact with Jesus Christ.

We Encounter Christ in the Seven Sacraments of the Church

The sacraments express the very way in which Christ accomplishes our redemption. He is the living Word who becomes a part of this world. He joins himself to human nature in order to transform it into an opportunity for people to once again come into contact with God the Father. In Christ, God acts through human action. The sacraments are profoundly meaningful symbolic human gestures which, when joined to the words of Jesus, bring us into direct contact with the life, meaning, and mission of Christ. They have the power to put us in intimate contact with the persons of the Trinity. Jesus instituted these sacraments during his life as a way to take the ordinary human activities we engage in throughout our lives and transform them into profound experiences of the gift of God's presence.

The seven sacraments can be classified according to what they do for those who receive them. God makes use of natural moments of human openness to become present to us in powerful ways. Since human beings are individuals that relate to each other socially, the sacraments are charged with meaning on many levels. They are not only sources of grace for the individual who receives them. They are also activities of the Church which enrich the entire Christian community each time any one of us receives them. They are celebrations that remind us of who we are as God's people, and they are what we do as God's people. There are sacraments of initiation which roughly parallel the growth process of human life and maturation; sacraments of healing which provide an opportunity for God to make contact with us when we are in need of forgiveness or help; and sacraments of lifetime commitment which become an opportunity for the awareness of God's presence and accompaniment in our life choices and the living out of our commitments. These different types of sacrament flow out of and back toward the central sacrament of the Eucharist, which reveals their truest meaning and provides the key to their proper understanding.

The Sacraments of Initiation

The sacraments baptism and confirmation are called sacraments of initiation, because they "initiate" the person who receives them into the life in Christ that we all share. Eucharist is also a sacrament of initiation, but because all the other sacraments are really directed toward the Eucharist, I have chosen to treat it separately from the others (pages 94-100).

Baptism

Baptism parallels human physical birth. It is a spiritual rebirth. This is one reason why in the Catholic Church we normally baptize infants. It is important not to fall into a dualistic perception that baptism is only about the soul. It's about the whole living human person, both body and soul. Baptism is about life—the next life yes—but also this life here and now. The human person is an individual, but one joined in relationship to others. Baptism is about the person receiving it and it is also about the Christian family, the Church. It is a time in which not only the baptized person is changed, but in which the entire Church is changed and enriched. The shared faith experience of the Church is enlarged and gifted in the baptism of every new member. In fact it is baptism which mysteriously joins this life to the next life for the person who receives it and joins this person's life to the lives of all other baptized persons, both living and dead.

By speaking the words of Jesus while performing the gesture of bathing with water, baptism produces three main effects. Baptism removes original sin and any personal sins; makes one a child of God by bringing about a new spiritual birth; and makes the person a member of God's people by incorporating the person into the Church. These three effects are the result of the gift of sanctifying grace. By way of the water, which symbolizes both death and life, the baptized person dies and rises with Christ. The Spirit of God begins to dwell inside that person. The newly baptized all bear within themselves the very life of God. They are born again into the realm of spirit and become a new creation. Just as at the baptism of Jesus, the heavens open, the Spirit of God descends, and the Father speaks. Though we only see these things with the eyes of faith, the Spirit of God does hover over the water. The voice of God the Father speaks to both the newly baptized and to all those present: "This is my son, my daughter, and I am pleased." The Divine Light present at the first moment of creation, who came into the world to cast out the darkness of sin and death, who himself died and rose to life, now makes himself present and enables the newly baptized to see what the living light in whom we put our faith reveals.

Baptism is a powerful spiritual moment which changes forever the person who receives it. But it is not a magic remedy for all problems or evils. It is only a beginning. It offers the person a wealth of new possibilities. It is now possible for the child to live in a way that was not possible prior to baptism. The baptized person now shares in the ministry of Christ and the Church. One is now anointed as priest, prophet, and king as Christ is. One's life ministry is to teach, govern, and sanctify as Christ does. But the child must still learn how to live these ministries and eventually will have to choose to live these things which baptism makes possible. The new life in Christ has to be nourished, protected, directed, and guided. This education into Christian living is of course the primary responsibility of both parents and godparents. Since it takes a village to raise a child well, it is also the job of the Christian community at the local parish level. The very role of parenting the baptized child becomes a source of grace for parents and godparents, as they also are brought into deeper relationship with Christ by introducing him to their children. To baptize a child and not teach its meaning, or help the child to live the power that it offers, is unfair to the child. It is a missed opportunity to experience God's grace for all of us.

Confirmation

Parents, godparents, the extended family, and the local parish community are all obligated to help the baptized to grow in knowledge and in spirit. This growth requires more than merely learning a few prayers or knowing a few of the teachings of the Church. They must learn the theology behind the prayers and the teachings, their meaning, and the reasons why we believe what we believe and pray the way we do. Growth also requires helping them to come to recognize the power and presence of God in the ordinary moments of life. As they learn to do these things, they grow in grace and wisdom. They come to understand what their Christian dignity is and what living this dignity requires of them. They reach a point in which they feel the need to confirm this faith.

We Catholics normally are baptized at birth, and the gift of baptism was given to us through another's consent in our name. As we attain maturity, it becomes necessary to say yes to the gift of grace with our own words and with our own will. Mature faith carries within itself the urge to make itself known. When we have truly encountered Christ, we feel the need to bring others to him. The sacrament of confirmation becomes the way in which the young person dialogues with God in a conversation of mutual commitment. The young Christians say to God that they believe, they love Jesus Christ, they value their personal relation with Christ as savior and guide, and that they will continue to live the faith with which they have been gifted throughout life. God confirms this commitment with a commitment of his own, given through the descent of the Holy Spirit and a new seven-fold gifting.

Through the laying on of hands by the bishop, who is the successor to the apostles, the same Holy Spirit that descended upon the apostles at the first Pentecost and brought the Church into being, now descends upon the one being confirmed, bearing seven powerful gifts of grace. These gifts of wisdom, fortitude, fear of the Lord, knowledge, counsel, understanding, and piety are powers which enable us to live more fully the meaning of our baptism. These solidify and strengthen the effects of baptism. They give a deeper appreciation and understanding of what following Christ means here and now in this life. They stir up in us a desire to live this way. The descent of the Spirit upon Jesus at his Transfiguration enabled him to see more clearly what being the Son of God required of him, fortifying him as he set his face like flint and headed toward Jerusalem to undergo crucifixion. The descent of the Spirit on the apostles at Pentecost enabled them to overcome their fear, leave the safety of the room in which they had locked themselves, and go out and proclaim the good news of Jesus' resurrection in words that others could understand. The spiritual gifts of the Holy Spirit enables these young persons to understand what being the son or daughter of God, which they became in baptism, requires of them now as adults, and gives them the strength, the courage, and the wisdom to live their commitment faithfully. In seeing their strength, hope, and love driving them to deeper commitment, the entire community present also is inspired to renew its own commitment.

The Sacraments of Healing and Forgiveness

Even though the power of original sin has been taken away by baptism, the effects of that sin upon our nature remain. Most people in this world try to do what is good and right in their daily lives, but wills are weak and reason has blind spots. We needn't be afraid of sin. We need not fall into despair over our own imperfection. Jesus provides for healing and forgiveness in the sacrament of reconciliation.

People become ill, grow old, experience pain, and die. Human suffering is both a challenge and a mystery to us. We read in the first chapter of the Book of Wisdom that God does not enjoy seeing people suffer. God never intended for people to experience pain or to die. And we also know that in Christ, God has resolved these issues for those who have received the gift of salvation. We know by faith that we are eternal and that life is everlasting. This knowledge of faith becomes real, experiential, and personal knowledge in the sacrament of the anointing of the sick.

Penance and Reconciliation

We don't always hit the target. We don't always get the point. Sooner or later most of us have to deal with the reality of sin in our lives and the painful consequences that result from our bad choices and our mistaken judgments. Relationships are damaged, hearts broken, lives wounded, shattered, and even destroyed. Some choices and actions are so serious in their nature and their effects that they are capable of severing completely our relationship with Christ and the Church. One of the central teachings of Jesus during his lifetime was the need for forgiveness. His ministry is one of reconciling humanity to God, and that ministry continues in and through his Church. He breathed upon his disciples and gave them his Spirit, conferring upon the Church the power to forgive sins. The desire of God to grace us in Christ is so powerful that even when we have lost sanctifying grace, when we have broken our relationship with God, when we have been blinded and weakened by sin, Christ still continues to gift us with the grace to see our sin, our need, to remember what we have lost, and to see the harm we have done to ourselves and to others. This grace moves us to seek forgiveness and reconciliation.

Jesus reminded us that unless we forgive our brothers and sisters from the heart, we should not expect forgiveness from our Father. Right relationship with God also requires a right relationship with other people who are God's image. Reconciliation with God and reconciliation with people go hand in hand. This is why we call the sacrament instituted by Christ to make this happen the sacrament of reconciliation. It is the way that we are forgiven and where we learn how to forgive, in which we are reconciled to God and to each other. The focus is on the power of God's love for us to heal.

This sacrament makes use of the most fundamental of all natural human symbols—the word. Words are by their nature social realities. They are spoken and heard, communicate meaning and are understood. In this sacrament the words express both meaning and feeling. "I have done wrong," and "I am sorry." The gesture is apology, conversation, dialogue, forgiveness. My sin wounds me, but it also wounds all others who are members of the body of Christ because I am a member of the body. I express the honest realization that I have done evil, brought about negative consequences, harmed others, and that this has harmed my relationship with God and his people. I ask for forgiveness and the priest, as representative of Christ and as representative of the Church, listens and in the name of Christ and all Christians everywhere who have been harmed by my sin, forgives and restores me to God's grace. I am not only reconciled to God, but to all of those who are one with God.

To be truly effective, reconciliation requires that we approach it with the proper state of mind and heart. We have to want to change for the better. We need to be honest in truly recognizing areas of weakness and failure. We have to come to the sacrament with a real intention to try to do better, with a true sorrow for having brought about harm, for having damaged our relationships, for having put the life of the spirit in danger. We must be willing to actively attempt to undue the damage caused by our sin by doing penance.

This experience of having been absolved of sin, when reflected upon seriously, has several powerful effects. It makes us more realistic about ourselves, about what we are and capable of doing, and thus it makes us more patently aware of the need for God's grace in our lives. It keeps us honest and makes us more understanding of others, since the gift of forgiveness carries with it an obligation to forgive as we have been forgiven. The recognition that we are decent people trying to do what is good, but who continue to occasionally fall also gives us hope, teaches us compassion for others, and serves as a remedy for the all too powerful aspect of original sin which rears its ugly head in the form of sitting in judgment over others. Finally, the very act of being forgiven restores and heals our relationship to God, restoring us to sanctifying grace or increasing its effects. In this way we become stronger and are given the concrete help to avoid falling into this or similar sins in the future. Through this sacrament's power, our very weakness is transformed into a source of greater strength.

Anointing of the Sick

Moments of serious illness turn our minds and thoughts to things that are important. They raise questions which are the result of facing our mortality. Has my life had meaning? Have I been a decent person? Is there anything that I have left undone? They also bring us face to face with the harshest reality. No matter how long I live, I will never be able to accomplish all that I dream of or attain all that I desire. No matter how hard I try, I will never be able to become exactly the person that I want to be. No matter how much I exercise, no matter how carefully I watch my diet, no matter how much medicine I take, or how much the sciences discover about how the body works, I will eventually succumb to sickness, aging, and death. At these difficult moments of self-reflection and answer seeking, Christ asks the Church to make itself present through the anointing of the sick. This presence becomes a living expression of the unity of the body of Christ. Every person's pain, suffering, illness, doubt, fear, search for meaning, is that of all of us. We stand with each other in our shared faith, and that faith motivates us to offer comfort and care.

The symbol of anointing consecrates one to the service of God as priest, prophet, and king. Anointing with oil is also symbolic of medicinal healing. The two meanings are brought together in this sacrament. We share in Christ's ministry. Christ heals. Now at a time of weakness, the individual who was anointed in baptism is anointed again and reminded that sharing in Christ's priesthood requires offering spiritual sacrifice to God. Uniting our pain to that of Christ on the cross in the sacrament enables it to attain a deeper meaning. We are now able to see that we are not suffering for nothing. Our pain, even our death, has salvific meaning. It is a way of exercising Christ's priesthood for the salvation of others. Here the prophetic role of suffering is also revealed. The very acceptance and struggle with illness becomes a living proclamation of God's call to embrace life, even in its most vulnerable moments. In bearing our sufferings with courage and hope, we also discover another aspect of the kingly ministry of Christ, that of dignity and power. Even Christ had to die. This is part of what it is to be truly human. Yet Christ voluntarily accepted this aspect of what it is to be human, with confidence that God the Father can and does bring life out of death. Through the power of the sacrament, the sick person discovers this same confidence and the graced dignity which flows from it. The sick become for those of us who are healthy a living sign of God's presence and activity around us, especially in those places where God seems to be most absent. The gift of hope and healing of the sacrament is directed primarily to those who are ill, but it flows beyond them and through them also to those who are well.

The healing flowing from this sacrament is twofold.

Often the person receives physical healing or a significant improvement. It is for this reason that the sacrament should not be thought of as something only for those at the moment of death and who are without hope or as a ritual that should only be given once. Anyone with any serious illness has both a right and a need for this sacrament because it is God's will that disease and sickness should be cured. There are times when a physical cure is not possible. In this case the sacrament prepares the individual to let go of this life and embrace eternity. In the anointing ritual, which also includes the sacraments of reconciliation and Eucharist, the recipient is assured that all is right with God and that entry into eternal happiness will be smooth and speedy. This calms the individual and transforms one of the most frightful, painful, and difficult moments of life into an opportunity for faith, thus bringing about the completion of a process of growth and development begun at baptism.

The Sacraments of Commitment and Service

The vocation of the disciple of Christ is a call to live the sanctifying grace received in the sacrament of baptism. The fundamental vocation of every follower of Jesus Christ is to love as God loves. We are chosen and called to live as Christ in this world. Christ's ministry is to be priest, prophet, and king. From these three ministries come the three fundamental activities of sanctifying, teaching, and governing. These are ways of loving God and neighbor. Every person is the unique image of God redeemed and saved by Christ, and so each individual will fulfill this vocation to love in his or her own particular and unique way. There are many ways to serve God and to bring others to knowledge of God's love in Christ. Christ provided us with two special sacraments, matrimony and holy orders, that were specifically designed to aid us in discovering the meaning of our baptismal vocation to love so that we can live this love effectively and evangelically in our daily lives.

These sacraments are not only for the benefit of those who receive them. They are given for the entire world. Not only clerics and married laity learn how to love. The unmarried and non-ordained also share in and benefit from these sacraments. When sacramentally ordained or married people live the grace these sacraments give, the entire Church receives their grace on a daily basis. We learn the meaning of God's love by the concrete example of those who embody this love. We all become more capable of loving as Christ loves.

Matrimony

The meaning and purpose of matrimony is revealed in the sacramental symbol which married life communicates. Marriage is a living symbol of the relationship between Christ and the Church, of the unity of humanity and divinity which is brought about in the person of Jesus, and the communion which Christ's love makes possible through the Church. When we look at the Christian family, we learn something unique about how God loves, about what it means to be a follower of Christ, and about what it means to authentically image God in this world.

Unlike the other six sacraments, in which the ordained priest administers the sacrament, the husband and wife themselves administer the sacrament of matrimony. The symbols used are words, and the gesture which provides the context of meaning for the words is the making of a promise. Husband and wife promise to build together "a full partnership of life and love." This partnership of love requires a total gift of self of each partner to the other. Making this total gift of self is loving as Jesus loves. It is the same way that Christ loves the human race. It is the same promise of love which Christ made with humanity in the new covenant that we celebrate in Eucharist. In loving each other this way, both man and woman discover Christ alive in each other.

Christian married love has its own unique quality. It is fully human. It is both a physical and a spiritual loving. It is expressed not only with words, feelings, and ideas, but also with gestures, with actions, with the body. Spirit and body must be joined in honest expression. This is why for a Catholic the act of sexual intercourse must always be an honest expression of love which commits itself to deeper love. As a total gift of self, nothing is held back. There is nothing left to give to any other person, nothing that is not shared, and so this love is faithful. This love as a total gift is a promise to love for a lifetime, in spite of any difficulties or unexpected challenges that may come. Married love in this sense is an act of faith. It is faith in the power of love to endure, to overcome any problem, difficulty, or obstacle. It is faith in the person loved. It is faith in the God who is source and protector of this love. And this love is creative and fruitful. It naturally grows and expands and seeks to share itself with others beyond the two persons who are loving. Love of this kind comes to its natural fulfillment and fruition in the creation of new life, offering new opportunities for love.

In this way of loving, which only the grace of God makes possible, husband and wife discover and begin to live God's original intention for the human race. Man and woman by their life of love together image God as male and female in complementarity and unity. In respecting each other's dignity and equality, in cooperating together to seek to know the God who is the source of their love, and in defining the form and shape of their lives together according to the God they discover through their love for each other, they become living signs of the power of salvation, and they become sources of hope for the world. By joining together in a relationship of love which results in the creation of new human life, in caring for and educating their children, in seeing them as the greatest blessing of their married love, they learn by experience what it is to image God the Creator in a powerful way unlike any other possible for human beings.

The Christian family is the result of loving in this way. It is the sacrament of matrimony grown to fullness and the fundamental way in which God graces our world. We first experience the love of God by being loved in the family. We learn how to discover the image and likeness of God in each brother and sister. The family is where we learn what it means to follow Christ, and where we receive the grace to do so. In learning how to forgive each other, in being patient with each other, in praying together, in starting over together after failing, in sustaining and strengthening each other's faults, etc., we learn the deeper and truer meaning of what real love is, as both joy and sacrifice. We not only come to understand the good news about Jesus that we are sent to proclaim, we become the living proclamation of this good news.

The family which results from loving in this way is the foundation of Church. Through the sacrament of matrimony, the family participates in the mission of the Church. People who see the way Catholics live as husband and wife, and as a wider family, come to understand who God is, what the coming of Christ means and makes possible, what human beings saved by Christ are able to become, and how living the Gospel of Jesus changes the world. In living the deepest meaning of their marriage vows as a true Christian family, husband and wife together teach the world about God by their example. They sanctify the world through their faithful and sacrificial loving as Christ loves. They govern the world as active participants in making the world a place where God's grace can be experienced by all people. When people see the way that Christian families live together, they see what it is to be an image and likeness of the true God in this world. They should ache with desire to have what God has given to us. The Christian couple who truly lives the sacrament of matrimony in its deeper meaning, becomes a living witness to salvation, a way that the Lord continues to draw all people to himself. The Christian family announces the Gospel of Jesus by the very way it lives and loves. In this way it doesn't only receive grace. The family becomes grace for the world.

Holy Orders

The Church's mission is to proclaim the good news that Jesus Christ has redeemed the human race, that Jesus wishes to draw all people to himself, and that those who come to him are transformed and made holy through the gift of salvation. It is in and through the Church that Christ's saving work continues. To accomplish this purpose, Jesus gathered apostles and handed his teaching on to them. By breathing his Spirit onto them, he gave them full authority to teach, govern, and sanctify in his name. He shared with them his mission in a unique way and sent them out to make believers of all nations. As the Church grew, the apostles passed on this power and authority to their successors and shared a portion of this power and authority with others who became their collaborators in the task of preaching the good news of Christ.

In our Church today, the bishops, as successors of these apostles, continue to exercise this unique authority to teach, govern, and sanctify by way of the sacrament of holy orders. Holy orders confers upon the one receiving it an indelible and permanent character. The recipient is consecrated, set apart for service to God's people. In order to fulfill the mission to serve God's people the ordained is given special graces which empower him to do things others cannot. These graces are not given for the welfare of the one ordained. They are given for the good of the Christian community, and they rightly belong to the Christian community. By way of this consecration, the person receiving the holy orders experiences Christ working through him within the ministry of service to God's people.

The grace of holy orders is transmitted through a laying on of hands by the bishop, combined with a prayer of consecration. There are three hierarchical levels of orders, each related to the ministry of service the person is called to perform. The fullness of holy orders resides in the bishop, whose ministry is to be the successor to the apostles. Then come the priests, who are ordained by the bishops to assist them in their ministry as apostles. Then come the deacons, whose role is to aid the bishops and priests in their ministry of service. Bishops carry the full power and authority given by Christ to the apostles through a direct and unbroken line of succession back to the time of the first twelve apostles.

Holy orders is a commitment to live out the meaning of baptism in a particular way. This sacrament is a commitment to a life of service, which complements the type of commitment made in matrimony. Holy orders is a total gift of self in service to the entire Christian community. Through holy orders, the recipient exercises the prophetic ministry of Christ by preaching and teaching the truths of the faith. He also exercises the priestly ministry of Christ by administering the sacraments to God's people. The minister exercises the kingly ministry of Christ by governing God's people in such a way that the common good of all the faithful is protected and by ensuring good order in the Christian community. Above all, the ordained encounters Christ in his life by becoming a presence of Christ to others in the exercise of his sacramental powers and his pastoral care of God's people. He discovers Christ by what Christ does through him. Just as Christ saved fallen humanity by entering into that very humanity and sharing life with us fully, the ordained exercises his ministry and experiences Christ by entering fully into the lives of the people that God has called him to serve. Rather than standing above others as holier, he discovers his holiness precisely through the experience of Christ's *kenosis*, as he serves God's people precisely as one of the people he is sent to serve.

At times fidelity to this calling requires prophetic confrontation. At other times, it brings joyous celebration. Sometimes it requires sharing sorrow and pain, bringing consolation and comfort. At all times it requires helping the people of God see the presence and activity of God all around us and discovering the meaning of what it is to follow Christ in the world today. By looking with the eyes of faith, by believing what faith reveals, by teaching what he believes, by living what he teaches, the ordained minister through his life of service becomes a living source of grace for God's people.

Eucharist—Center of the Church's Life

Eucharist is the sacrament around which the other six revolve. It is food for the journey of life. It is a memorial and a joining of oneself to the very sacrificial act of love which makes salvation possible. Above all, it is an act of gratitude. The word Eucharist stems from the Greek word meaning "Thank you." Eucharist is our way as individuals and as a people to express our gratitude to God the Father for the redemption that has been given to us as a gift in the person of Jesus Christ. The primary symbols used in Eucharist are bread and wine. The gesture which accompanies them is that of eating and drinking. The words which are joined to the gesture are those of Jesus, spoken on the night before his death, when gathered together with his disciples.

Bread is a powerful natural symbol. Bread is food. Without food there is no continuation of life. So bread first and foremost symbolizes life. But bread is not just any food. Bread is made of grain, crushed and joined together in such a way that it is impossible to distinguish where one grain begins and another ends. Bread symbolizes the unity of many grains made one for the purpose of nourishment. Grain in its own right is itself a powerful symbol, because the portion of the grain that becomes food is the germ, the seed of the wheat plant. The future life of the plant is sacrificed. The wheat stalk gives up both its present and its future life so that another being who eats can continue to live. So bread is also a symbol of sacrifice, of giving up one's present and one's future for the sake of another. Bread also has a rich human history. The domestication of wheat made the transition from a life of hunting and gathering to a life of dwelling in cities possible. Those who live by hunting must always be on the move. Wheat stays in one place. One person can grow enough wheat to feed hundreds of people. Wheat can be stored. Once humanity discovered how to make bread, civilized life with all of its consequences became possible for human beings. Bread is also a symbol of civilized life together as human beings.

Wine also has deep symbolic power. It is the blood of grapes. The grape when crushed is emptied completely of what makes it what it is. But the juice doesn't remain juice. It ferments, it changes into something else. In its new form it can enhance, even produce feelings of joy. When misused it can lead to sorrow and disaster. It has the power to cause one to lose control. But the ancients also believed that it had the power to elicit the truth and to produce visions. Wine is symbolic of blood, an emptying of self so another's thirst might be quenched, of transformation, and a source of truth, joy, and celebration.

Eucharist is also a symbol of freedom and unity which can only be appreciated in the light of God's activity throughout history. During their sojourn in Egypt, the Jewish people lived in a state of slavery. God called Moses to set them free by way of a lengthy process involving signs and wonders. But the end result of this process of liberation was the making of a covenant between God and people. This covenant merged the twelve distinct tribes of Israel into one people, established a formal relationship between them and God, and gave them a unique identity, the knowledge of who they were and how they were to live.

In making the covenant between God and the people of Israel at Mount Sinai, Moses made use of a unique ceremony. He presented them with the law which God had written for them as a guide for their behavior. He then invited all those who were willing to abide by the law and who wished to enter into covenant with their God to come forward. He slaughtered bulls as sacrificial victims, collecting their blood in bowls. He sprinkled the people with the remaining blood of the victim to symbolize that now they were all one blood and that each of their lives was now one with the life of the people and with the very life of their God. They then ate the flesh of the sacrificed bulls symbolizing they were one life and one flesh through eating the victim sacrificed and accepted by their God. By the power of the sacrifice, they ceased being a group of distinct tribes and were forged into a new civilization by the covenant. They became a nation with their own identity, which was communicated, expressed, and carried in the law that made them different from all other nations. From this point forward in their history, whenever the people sinned by violating the precepts of the covenant, they began to lose their identity as a people, their social life disintegrated into chaos, and personal and group suffering was the result. When turning back to the God who had made them his own, the covenant was reenacted and renewed by the making of sacrifices. Reenacting the covenant sacrifice of Sinai became a way of remembering who they were, of how God had freed them from slavery and forged them into his people. It also became a way of seeking reconciliation and restoration, and renewing their commitment to live as God's Chosen People.

Jesus takes the powerful natural meanings already present in bread and wine, and he joins them to the religious meaning of covenant sacrifice to bring about a new way for us to come into direct personal contact with his saving life and mission. On the night before he dies he takes the bread and wine and he offers them to God. His life and God the Father's, which are already one, are now joined symbolically to the bread and wine. By the power of his words he then transforms them into his own life and offers this life to his disciples whom he loves. The bread becomes his body. The wine becomes his blood. As he breaks the bread he is symbolically telling them what will happen to his body the next day. It will be broken and torn. As he pours the wine out into a bowl, he is symbolically telling them that the next day the blood will pour out of his own body. He himself is the bread broken and the wine poured out as he mounts the cross. And when they see it happen the next afternoon they are to remember that he is doing this for them. And as he invites them to eat his flesh and drink his blood, he offers them a share in his own life. He makes a new covenant with them, merges them into a new people, gives them a new identity, provides them with a new law, begins in them the building of a new civilization. Now they are one with him. As he dies and rises, they will also share in his death and resurrection. This is how they and all humanity will be reconciled to God the Father through Jesus, by way of the oneness brought about by the power of this sacrament.

The sacrament of the Eucharist is the clearest and most perfect expression of salvation. When we eat the flesh and drink the blood of the Lord, we become both physically and spiritually one with the person of Jesus Christ. Since Jesus is one with the Father and the Spirit, we are drawn intimately into the very life and love of the Divine Trinity. And since there is only one God, and one Christ, we are also joined in unity to every other human being who is in union with that one God. For this reason Eucharist is often called Communion, a word which in its Latin root means "to unite." We are all one life, and that life is Christ. This is why only believing Catholics are invited to receive Communion at a Catholic Mass, and why some Catholics, because of their condition in life at a given moment, should not take Communion. To engage in a symbolic activity which expresses unity of belief and life when this unity of belief and life does not exist in reality is to express something which is untrue. On the other hand, unless we regularly express our desire for this unity of life, and seek out its source, it will never become a reality for us. By joining our lives to the life of Christ crucified and risen, and putting us into direct contact with the act of redemption itself, the Eucharist removes the power of sin over our lives. It reminds us of the source of our freedom and it is what keeps us free.

Eucharist is also the renewal of the covenant made between humanity and God the Father through the sacrifice of Christ. It is a banquet in which we reenact symbolically and mysteriously the one sacrifice of Christ and celebrate as a community what God has done for us. By eating the flesh of the victim, like the people of Israel did at Sinai, we unite our own sacrifices, our hopes and fears, our pains and joys, to Christ's one sacrifice, asking him to transform us into something greater. We celebrate the identity and the dignity that being God's people confers upon us. We remember who we are called to become in this world and are given the power to become what God is calling us to be. Eucharist makes it possible for us to continue building the new civilization, the new humanity which Christ came to this earth to make possible. It creates the Catholic Church. He is the bread which nourishes our life as a Church and as children of God. He is the wine which ferments within us and transforms us as we grow in holiness. He is the bread and wine which becomes for us the source of our celebration and joy, which provides us with a knowledge of what is true and reduces the human inhibitions which enslave and misguide us. He is the bread which makes us who we are, and who educates us about what being children of God means and requires of us. He is the bread and wine which lays down his temporal life, which allows himself to be crushed, so that we might be set free from the slavery of sin and have a future of eternal happiness. Eucharist transports us back powerfully in memory and places us in direct contact with that moment in human history which changed humanity forever. It unites us to the ongoing work of redemption. It is our renewal and recommitment to for us, in producing bodily and spiritual healing or in preparing us for eternal life and entry into the happiness prepared for us and willed for us by the Father. For this reason, the Eucharist is often combined with the anointing as *Viaticum*, or food for the journey, which reminds us that there is nothing to fear. Christ has conquered death. Matrimony and holy orders, as life callings, celebrate the living out daily of the meaning of Eucharist. Eucharist reveals to us what it means for us as individuals and as a Church to be faithful to our calling and gives us the power to live authentically this calling. As married people raising a family, or as ordained ministers to others, we transform this world into the kingdom of heaven by tangibly living what it means to eat the flesh and drink the blood of Jesus Christ.

We receive the gift of God's grace freely in the sacraments and in other ways, but the gift is not a magic medicine for solving all of our problems. We have to cooperate with grace, and we have to learn how to use it properly or we can lose it. Saint Timothy himself had to be reminded by Saint Paul "rekindle the gift of God" he had received (2 Timothy 1:7). The more we cooperate with grace, the more effective it becomes. Grace is God's love for us which enables us to love God and other people in return. The change brought about in us by grace is a change which effects the entire world in which we live. It flows out of our individual lives into the way we live in relationship with others, the place we have in this world, the choices we make, and the actions which flow out of them.

Chapter Four

Living the Faith that Understands Itself

Theological reflection is one of the ways to stir grace into flame. The theology of salvation immediately reveals two necessary avenues that must be joined together for grace to become truly effective. Grace is the experience of God's loving presence in our lives. God is revealed by word and action. We stir up the grace of God by word and action, prayer, and moral living. God's word and action become one and the same coherent thing in the person of Jesus Christ. And so, when our words and actions, our prayer and our moral life have also become one coherent reality, the grace of God's salvation becomes powerfully manifested in our own experience, and we become living signs of hope and witnesses to the world of what God has done for us in Jesus the Christ.

1. Stirring the Gift into Flame through Prayer

God is intimately experienced in prayer as conversation. Prayer can be either private or public, devotional or liturgical, personal or communal. These are all necessary ways of praying. We can create a god of our own imagination, an idolatry of the mind in prayer which is always and only private. The human mind can play tricks on us. We can mistake a feeling, a sound, an experience which is merely the product of our own imagination for the presence of God. So it's necessary to pray with others as well. There is also a deeper reason. Salvation comes to us not just as individuals, but also as members of a community. Grace appears most clearly and powerfully through our membership in the Church and when we pray as a community. Jesus made the promise that whenever two or three would gather together in his name, he would be present to them. There is only one Christ, and a relationship with the one Christ joins all of us who are related to him into the same relationship of oneness. Praying together publicly as a community of believers deepens this shared relationship with Christ and others. In Christ, "me and God" becomes "we in God."

Each of our life situations, our abilities, our thoughts and dreams are uniquely our own. There is no aspect of our lives that cannot be brought to God in prayer. There are things that are private and personal that we need to share and discuss with the Lord. Our public prayer must also be complemented by private prayer. Private prayer prepares us for greater and more meaningful participation in shared public prayer, and our shared public prayer provides us with inspiration for our private prayer. We should pray as individuals in private for others, and we must pray in public as a group for the individuals in our midst who are in need of our prayers.

The Effects of Prayer

All prayer is beneficial if done well. The actual form that our prayer takes is not as important as the spirit with which we approach prayer. We need to want to converse with God. Authentic prayer should not be thought of as a painful obligation, but rather as a joyous privilege, an opportunity to which we look forward. This does not mean that prayer is always experienced as joyful. Our prayer must also be honest. Those who worship God must worship in spirit and truth. Sometimes prayer requires of us that we face unpleasant truths about ourselves. At times in prayer God shows us things about ourselves that we would rather not deal with. Sometimes it is difficult to pray. Often the most beneficial moments of prayer in terms of real grace are those which force us to break out of our comfort zones, face harsh truth, shatter the lies we have created about ourselves to protect our self-esteem and comfort. At times God just tells us to shut up and listen, and when we try to pray, the words stick in our throats. Sometimes the mere desire to pray is the only prayer we are able to summon. But that honest desire to pray is still prayer.

All prayer is heard by God. All prayers are answered. The answer we receive may not always be what we are expecting, and we may not always receive what we are asking for. Sometimes the answer is silence. We must remember the words of Jesus, that our heavenly Father will give us only good things, those things we really need to help us (Matthew 7:11). Observing what we do not receive when we ask, and what we do receive even when we haven't asked, becomes a method of learning what it is that we really need, what is truly good, and what is really helpful in living life as a follower of Christ. In this way prayer frees us from illusions and delusions about what is of real importance in life, and this enlightenment in itself is a powerful grace.

Forms of Prayer

Specific prayer forms have been handed down from generation to generation because they identify and unite us as a unique Church and because they are extremely effective in stirring up the power of salvation. The first prayers we learn as children are formula prayers which join together many different ways of praying. The Our Father was Jesus' answer to the request of the apostles to teach them how to pray. It combines many different types of praying into one integrated whole. The words we speak remind us that we are all God's children, that God watches over, forgives us, protects us, and that we are called to recognize the Father's holiness by doing God's will on earth and by forgiving each other as God has forgiven us. The Hail Mary reminds us of the words spoken to Mary by the angel Gabriel. These words were God's invitation to her to make the act of faith which transformed her into the mother of the Lord. When we say these words that were spoken to Mary who is our model for faith and join them to our request that she pray for us, we are asking for the gift to be able to respond to God's call to us in the same spirit and with the same answer that she gave. The Glory Be is a traditional formula giving praise to each of the three persons of the Blessed Trinity.

The only danger in using these formula prayers is the possibility of becoming so familiar with them that we fall into the sheer repetition of words without really thinking about what we are saying. The challenge of praying in this way is to ensure that we do so intentionally, consciously aware of what the words mean, so that the prayer can do for us what it is truly capable of doing. Prayer is conversation with God. In speaking to the Lord, we should know what we are saying, and we should mean what we say. Ultimately these simple patterned prayer forms, which are very useful for public and shared praying, lead us into a more mature and personal way of praying.

Aids in Prayer

In our prayers we Catholics often make use of sacramentals such as holy pictures, medals, candles, icons, or other images of the saints, the crucifix, palms, and ashes. These are tangible symbols which point our minds to holy realities, placing us into a mental framework in which we are better prepared to recognize the presence of God and converse more honestly with God. They have no power to confer grace in themselves, but they do focus our mental prayer on the realities expressed and brought about by the seven sacraments. They remind us of who we are and who we are called to become. If not properly understood they might mistakenly appear to be Catholic "good luck charms" or magical amulets or talismans. But the sacramentals, when correctly understood, are simply human artifacts which help turn the mind toward the realities of faith.

Catholics also honor the Mother of Jesus and the other saints in prayer. In reality, this ancient tradition in our Church is nothing more than the recognition of the unity of all the faithful, and an act of faith in the resurrection of Jesus. There is continuity between this world and the next. Life in Christ is in fact eternal. Those who have died in the peace of Christ are still alive in and with Christ. And in and through the Church as the living mystical body of Christ, and as the pilgrim people of God, we are able to communicate with them and they with us. They have already arrived at the place to which we are all journeying. They have been successful in the Christian life. We do not pray to them to them as if they were God, or as a substitute for praying to God. This kind of prayer is similar to speaking to one's grandfather and asking for help or guidance in a difficult situation. It is nothing more than a request for them to pray for us or to help us, in much the same way that we pray for each other and ask each other for help. Mary is the perfect model of what it means to be a follower of Christ who does the will of God, and there is no one who can give us better advice about how to serve God, about how to bear Christ in our lives and bring others to him, than the woman whose entire life is defined by that vocation.

2. The Mass—The Prayer of the Catholic Church

The greatest and most powerful prayer of all for the Catholic is the Mass. Never private, it is always public. Never individual, it is always a group activity. It is in fact the prayer that most powerfully and perfectly expresses the meaning of what it is to be Christ's body, and the very reason for the existence of the Catholic Church. It is the celebration of who we are and what we are called to do. Christ founded the Church to continue his ongoing work of salvation until his return at the end of time. The Church is where people encounter Christ, so that Christ can bring them into intimate contact with God the Father. This is the work of all of the members of the Church understood in its widest sense, which includes all baptized believers, living and dead. There is a longstanding spiritual tradition which holds that each time a Christian community gathers to celebrate the Mass, the entire mystical body of Christ is present, uniting our offerings and prayers here on earth to the eternal offering of praise which the saints in heaven engage in constantly. Mass is a taste of heaven on earth for those who have the vision to see. But it is not only about experiencing heaven or uniting earth to heaven. Wherever two or three are gathered in his name, Christ is present. Where Christ is present, his power and his mission of salvation continue. Where Christ is present, the whole Church is present. This is the theological reason why the Mass is always a community celebration. Community is one of the first and foremost ways in which Christ becomes present to us. We experience Christ present in the community which gathers to celebrate and worship as God's people joined together as one in Christ.

The Mass, as our prayer to God the Father, unites all three of the ways in which Christ becomes present to us: community, word, and Eucharist. The word Mass, stemming from the Latin root *missa* means "to be sent," and expresses what we are celebrating and praying for. We prepare ourselves for our mission in this world, which is nothing more or less than to become ever more effective images of God in this world. By doing this, we transform this world into God's kingdom. We are part of this world. As we change through our contact with Christ, the world changes through us. Since this mission is that of Christ, it is precisely in our communing with Christ in his multiple forms of presence that we receive the knowledge, ability, and strength of will to live what we are celebrating as we leave the Church and return to our daily activities. In the Mass, we renew the covenant that Christ has made between God and humanity and we celebrate the freedom that his sacrifice has accomplished in us. By eating his body and drinking his blood, Christ nourishes us giving us strength to accomplish the task we are sent out to do. He reminds us of who we are, our shared history as a people, and the future history we are called to construct by our choices and actions, not only for ourselves as Church, but for all of humanity, proclaiming the good news and making believers of all peoples.

Introductory Rites

The Mass begins and ends with the making of the Sign of the Cross, identifying all present as followers of the Lord and helping us to focus our minds on the meaning of what we are about to do. We engage in a short expression of recognition of our fallen human state and the power that sin has over human lives, preparing ourselves mentally, emotionally, and spiritually to celebrate what Christ does for us. We confess that we are in need of the gift of salvation. We admit and recognize that we need the prayers of others and that we have the obligation to aid others with our prayers. We make an act of faith and gratitude pointing forward to what Christ does for us in the celebration of word and Eucharist. He sets us free from the power of sin by joining us to himself.

Liturgy of the Word

During the Liturgy of the Word, Christ becomes powerfully present through the revealed Word of God. Christ is the word of God made flesh, the same Word revealed in the sacred Scriptures. Any time that we read the Bible, we encounter Christ present to us. When we gather together to do so, we become more fully aware and better able to appreciate this presence, what it means for us as a people, and what it demands of us. A person who participates actively in daily Mass over the course of a three-year period will have heard and meditated upon all of the most important revelatory passages contained in the sacred Scriptures. In the Catholic liturgy we read two scriptural passages on weekdays and three on Sunday. On Sunday, one reading is taken from the Old Testament, one from the New Testament books other than the gospels, and one from the gospels. The central focus is upon the gospel, the other two readings being used in order to understand more deeply the meaning of the good news. The Scriptures are then explained to us by the Church's ordained minister whose sacramental ministry it is to help us understand what God is saying to us here and now.

The community responds to the word of God by making an act of faith which links us to all Christians from the beginning of the Church up until the present. Through recitation of the fundamental truths of our faith contained in the Nicene Creed, we express and renew our solidarity with those who have gone before us and all other Catholics. The Creed is our community response to Christ present in the word that reminds us of our identity as Christ's followers and as members of his body. It is our way of saying "Yes, Lord, we believe," to what we have just heard. Doing this prepares us to encounter Christ in the more intimate presence of the sacrament of the Eucharist.

Liturgy of the Eucharist

The Liturgy of the Eucharist begins with the preparation of the gifts of bread and wine during which time a collection is normally taken up from those present. This money goes to assure that we as a community are able to continue to have a place in which to celebrate Mass. It also reminds us that the only reason we still have a parish Church in which to encounter the presence of Christ today is because others before us gave as we are giving now. We now give so that our children and grandchildren will continue to have the privilege of this place and the opportunity to receive what we are receiving at this moment. Rather than giving to God, the collection is ensuring that God will be able to continue to give to us and those who come after us. The collection is also a symbolic way in which each individual joins his or her personal sacrifices to the bread and wine which will be offered to God and transformed into the Body and Blood of Jesus. It is the way in which we unite all of our own personal sacrifices, desires, fears, hopes, and dreams to the one sacrifice of Christ, so that we can be united with him and be drawn up into the very mystery of his redemptive action.

The eucharistic prayer is prefaced with a response of the congregation acknowledging the holiness of God and recognizing that the one who comes in the name of the Lord is blessed. This of course reminds us not only of the triumphal entry of Jesus into Jerusalem on Palm Sunday, but also of the words of Jesus in the gospel, that we would not see him again until we were able to say "Blessed is the one who comes in the name of the Lord" (Luke 13:35). Our saying of these words is our recognition that he is our Lord and Savior and that we are about to see him. The eucharistic prayer which follows is divided into three sections: the *anamnesis*, or the remembering of God's actions in our history; the *epiclesis,* or the calling down of the Holy Spirit; and the words of institution spoken by Jesus at the Last Supper. We remember all that God has done for humanity throughout history. We give thanks. We ask the Father to send the Holy Spirit to transform bread and wine into the Body and Blood of Jesus. By speaking the words of institution spoken by Jesus at his Last Supper, the miracle of transubstantiation is brought about by the Holy Spirit. The bread and wine, while continuing to appear as bread and wine, are really transformed into the Body and Blood of Christ. With Christ present upon the altar we now pray for those living and dead who are still in need of his forgiveness, redemption, and salvation. We end the eucharistic prayer with a great amen, affirming our desire that all glory and honor be given to the Father through the Son and the Spirit. This is our promise to turn away from all other idols which would serve to take glory away from our God. It is also our promise to live as God's image in the authentic way made possible by Christ present on the altar at that moment.

Communion Rite

The Lord's Prayer summarizes everything we are and want to be as God's people and reminds us what it is to be a follower and imitator of Jesus. It reminds us that the Jesus we are about to receive is the one who teaches us how to pray authentically. The prayer is followed by a sign of peace which expresses our unity, love, and concern. At a deeper level, the sign of peace expresses what is about to happen when we eat the flesh and drink the blood of Christ. We are going to be united into oneness not only with Jesus and the Trinity, but also with every other person who is united to the one Christ in that moment. If we are unable to turn to others in cordiality, we are not ready to experience oneness with them. The sign of peace readies us mentally and spiritually to really understand and experience the depth and breadth of Communion. It is me and Jesus, God the Father, the Holy Spirit, and all the other people in this room and throughout the world, the living and the dead, who dwell in unity with Christ.

We are what we eat and drink. Reception of the Body and Blood of Jesus transforms us into the Body of Christ. We become more perfectly the image of God, both as individuals and as a people. Eucharist forgives and casts out sin, because where Christ is present sin cannot endure. Eucharist strengthens our relationships, illuminates our vision to see ourselves as we truly are, and gives us the power to enter into deeper conversion of mind and heart. It makes being Christian a reality for us. But it can only do this if we truly and willingly believe in its power and want this to happen.

Communion is followed by a brief period of thanksgiving during which time we should remember the meaning of what has just happened. But we should also attempt to feel the experience, to enjoy the oneness with God and others. We should also remember to pray for those who are not able yet to have access to this experience, and for those who, for one reason or another, have lost the privilege, that they may experience the gift of God's presence in other ways and be speedily returned to Communion with us in the sacrament.

Concluding Rite

The Mass ends with our being sent forth in blessing. The priest or deacon speaks in the name of both Christ and the Church and invites us to go forth in peace to love and serve the Lord. As we leave the confines of the church building behind, we are to take what we have experienced and celebrated in the Mass and continue to make it real by our concrete choices and actions. We are to live what we have celebrated. We are to build the kingdom of God as individuals and as a Church. We are to live as members of the new civilization brought about on earth through the power of the Eucharist. This call to live the faith we celebrate is the root and heart of all Christian morality.

3. Living the Faith as Christian Companionship and Witness

In prayer we converse and commune with God and discover the meaning of grace. When we act upon the meaning of the grace we have received, the power of that grace increases. We again see this illustrated in Jesus' baptismal experience as recorded in Luke's Gospel. After hearing the Father's voice, Jesus is immediately led by the Holy Spirit into the desert to fast and pray. He prays about what he has just experienced. But he doesn't only pray. He also struggles with his own humanity. Knowledge of who he is requires a decision about how to live. He is tempted by the cunning one just as Eve was. But unlike Eve, who chose to put her faith in the false promise of a lie, Jesus looks to the presence, power, and grace of his Father's Spirit. He resists and overcomes the darkest temptations of human nature: the hunger for fame, power, and glory; the temptation to use his power for evil; to give in to the seduction of death. That is not what it means to be a child of the true God. Having discovered in prayer what it means to be God's Son, he doesn't just bask in the joy of his private knowledge. He immediately comes out of the desert, goes directly to the synagogue, and publicly announces the meaning of his baptismal experience of grace. He has to share the gift that he has been given with others. He is sent to bring good news to the poor, to set the captives free, to heal the lame, to bring sight to the blind. His public ministry begins as he starts to put the meaning of his graced event into practice by doing just these things. He becomes a living embodiment of God's love. God's words and deeds become the same thing in him. His life becomes a source of God's grace for others.

When we appreciate the deeper reality behind the visible celebration of the sacraments, and the power of prayer, then the saving grace of Christ we encounter in the sacraments flows outward and continues beyond the actual moment. One commits himself or herself not only to receive the gift of sanctifying grace, but to live its meaning. The sacraments in this broader sense define for us a specific and authentic way of living as redeemed and transformed human beings. They give form, shape, and meaning to our lives. We aren't just people who were baptized. We strive to live what our baptism means at every moment of our lives. We aren't just a couple who were married in Church. We live our sacramental marriage vows every day in such a way that we become living examples of the power and presence of God's love. By living the meaning of the seven sacraments within the Church, we become authentic "likenesses" of the God who calls all people to receive the gift of salvation. We each become the way in which Christ continues to call out to those in need of God's grace, and the way in which Christ graces them. And by doing this day after day, God acts through us and changes the world through our fidelity.

Understanding in Search of Fidelity

When faith arrives at the deeper understanding of this experience of God that a personal relationship with Christ provides, then theology as "faith in search of understanding" is inevitably transformed into "understanding in search of fidelity." We experience a powerful urge to concretely live what we have come to understand. In seeing how Christ brings the two sources of God's revelation together in his own person, as both word and action joined together in perfect unity, we realize that our vocation as Christ's followers is to live our lives in that same way. This is what it means to be images of the true God, whose words and deeds are never contradictory. The words of our belief have to be incarnated in our deeds. We see the real meaning of Saint James' teaching that faith without works is dead (James 2:14-26).

For the follower of Christ, morality is not a burden. It is a privileged vocation. We do not obey the commandments, or follow the teachings of Christ, or live the precepts of the Catholic Church in order to get a reward or to avoid a punishment. We don't do good and avoid evil because we're afraid that we'll go to hell if we don't or because we'll go to heaven if we do. We do what is good and right because that is the only fitting way to respond in gratitude to the God who has created us in his own image and likeness and has redeemed and saved us in the gift of Jesus Christ. We avoid evil because we know that doing evil is the very perversion and destruction of who and what we are. To do evil is to betray the very source of peace and joy of our lives. Moral life is a way of living the understanding we have gained by faith. It's not just what we do. It's who we are.

The Christian Moral Life

Christian morality is not about control and security nor about making sure people behave themselves. It's not about becoming perfect or a way to find God. It's the result of having found God in the person of Jesus. It's realizing that we can't ever be perfect, and so we need to open ourselves to Christ and cooperate with God's process of making us better. It's about learning how to live our freedom as God's people in ways that authentically image the God who created and loves us. It's about becoming living examples of what is possible for human beings in this world when they turn their minds and hearts to Christ. It's a response to God in thanksgiving for the gift of salvation we have received in Jesus. It's using the power God has given us. It's faithfully living the gift of faith which has restored us to our original dignity in the new creation. It's the way we announce and become announcements of the good news that salvation has come.

In Christ, the perfect image of the Father, we discover that there are two dimensions to our moral response. The vertical dimension of morality reminds us that we were created to be the image of God in this world. We are a way in which God becomes present in this world. The meaning and form of our existence is defined by the God whose image we are, and not by our own wants and wishes. We are created to give glory to God, not to amass glory for ourselves. So we need to keep our eyes, minds, and hearts focused on Christ as perfect image of the Father lest we forget who and what we are. God creates, and everything that God creates is good. Fidelity requires that we live our own ability to create by way of our concrete choices and actions, so that we authentically image God by creating what is good, rather than destroying or perverting the goodness that God has created. As thinking, reasoning beings this requires that we develop our minds and hearts so that we can distinguish correctly between those things which are good and those which are not. It requires the development of a healthy and well-formed moral conscience.

The horizontal dimension of our moral response reminds us that God is relational. Father, Son, and Spirit dwell in a relationship of love. To image God is to love. But God loves us in a particular way. God created us as a human race, individuals who join together in relationship, male and female in equal dignity and complementarity, different races and nations. God becomes one with all of us in Christ, draws us together into a people, and speaks and acts to and through that people. Christ wants all people to be saved. We are called to love each other and cooperate with each other the way Father, Son, and Spirit love each other and dwell together in unity. Christ manifests the Father's love as sacrifice for the well-being, redemption, and healing of the other. He cures the sick, feeds the hungry, drives the evil spirits away, and defends the dignity of the poor and the outcast. Our response of faith can do no less. Christ dies not only for the just, but for the unjust; not only for the good, but for sinners as well. God's justice in Jesus has been shown as mercy to us, and so we understand that we are called to manifest God's justice by showing mercy and forgiveness to others.

The Christian moral life as a concrete embodiment of the meaning of the cross of Christ brings these two dimensions, the horizontal and the vertical, into unity. Faith in Christ, when it attains understanding, discovers that it is not possible to love God without loving people. What we do to the least of our brothers and sisters we do to God. What we do here on earth has ramifications for eternity. We pray that God's will may be done here among us, as it is already being done in heaven. We ask for forgiveness to the same extent that we show forgiveness to others. Only those who actually hear the word of God and put it into practice will enter into the kingdom of God. But when people enter into the kingdom of God then the words of Jesus remain true and alive in this world. We find the answer to the questions asked earlier about what God is doing in the death of a starving child or the destruction of a city by a tsunami. God is helping them, feeding them, clothing them, healing them, sheltering them through us. God is inviting and challenging us to be his image and likeness to these people. We not only become the place where God becomes present in this world. We become the ways in which God speaks and acts in this world to communicate his redeeming and saving love. We become the vehicles of God's actual and saving grace in a world that still searches for the true face of its Creator.

The horizontal and vertical dimensions of Christian moral living as faith in practice come together powerfully in the Church. Here we, as followers of the same Lord, join together as individual believers in a relationship of faith for the purpose of imaging the God who has redeemed and saved us. In the Church we encounter Christ, who reveals to us what it means to be an authentic image of God in this world. God draws us together and, through the power of grace, of presence in community, word and sacrament, forms us into God's people. We are a force and a presence through which God acts in this world to continue the work of salvation. In our local parish life, we build the kingdom of God together, announcing the good news of what God has made possible for people in Christ by both word in deed. Here we discover the positive

Concluding Thoughts

There is a reason and a meaning for everything we do as Catholics. When we understand the reasons behind what we do and practice our faith in order to express these deeper meanings, our practices not only take on a more intentional quality, but the quality of the experience of faith itself changes and becomes much more profound, enriching, and enlightening. We begin to understand what we worship. True appreciation of this kind requires a lifelong process of prayer, reflection, and practice. Faith seeks understanding. Understanding seeks enlightenment and expression in prayer. Prayerful understanding flows outward into Church fellowship. Church fellowship informs and animates Christian moral life. Christian moral life becomes a new experience of faith in God's presence and power. That new experience of faith seeks further understanding. The process repeats itself again and again, and the gift of God that theology is continues until we find the understanding that faith is constantly seeking. But we don't only understand the words. In the search of faith, we actually discover that the words of Scripture have become a part of who and what we are:

So then you are no longer strangers and aliens, but you are citizens with the saints and also members of the household of God, built upon the foundation of the apostles and prophets, with Christ Jesus himself as the cornerstone. In him the whole structure is joined together and grows into a holy temple in the Lord; in whom you also are built together spiritually into a dwelling place for God.

EPHESIANS 2:19-22

Index